"This may be one of the most helpful books you read this year. I'm so grateful Jeannie has taken on the writing of this message that although it is theologically deep, is also completely able to be understood and applied. The topic of the Holy Spirit for most of us has seemed more like a mystery than a gift, but this book will change that in the most wonderful way."

—Lysa TerKeurst, #1 *New York Times* bestselling author of *Forgiving What You Can't Forget* and president of Proverbs 31 Ministries

"In *Don't Miss Out*, my dearest friend Jeannie will become yours as she leans in and gently whispers to you, 'Hey, that fifth gear you've been running on—the one that exhausts you—there is a better one. One that comes from within. It's been there all along; it's there to help and is fully available to you. It's the help you did not even know you could ask for. Don't miss out!' When you read this book, two things will happen: You will understand why I count myself blessed to call Jeannie my friend, and you will unlock the way you move through your day powered on WITHINfluence. Meet Jeannie—and our help, the Holy Spirit."

—Elisabeth Hasselbeck

"If you're going to read about the Holy Spirit, pick an author who has spent time with our Friend, Comforter, and Companion. If you're going to read about the Holy Spirit, pick an author who is gracious and generous and kind. If you're going to read about the Holy Spirit, pick a book that invites and encourages you to experience God—not just gain head knowledge about Him. Jeannie Cunnion is that author, and this is that book. I can't suggest it enough. *Don't Miss Out*, amen?"

—Jess Connolly, author of *You Are the Girl for the Job* and *Breaking Free from Body Shame*

"Jeannie had me laughing and crying and feeling the full range of human emotion. I've studied the t

extensively throughout my academic career, and I feel like I have a good grasp on the various nuances. But as I read *Don't Miss Out*, the Holy Spirit captured my heart. I found myself exalting the Father and marveling at the work of the Son all while being enamored by the glory, power, and presence of the Spirit. Thank you, Jeannie, for this very hard but tremendously holy work!"

—Joel Muddamalle, director of theology and research,
Proverbs 31 Ministries

"A must-read for anyone who feels a bit alone, not enough, unable, and not up to the task at hand. Jeannie graciously shares about the gift we have in the Holy Spirit. You will come away feeling so encouraged, comforted, and confident in what God is calling you to!"

—Alyssa Bethke, author of *Spoken For* and *Love That Lasts*

"Prepare to be blown away by what the Holy Spirit can do in and through you! My dearest friend Jeannie Cunnion shows you how personal and approachable the third member of the Trinity truly is. If you want to experience the fullness of God, if you want to experience all of God, don't miss out on this book!"

—Paula Faris, journalist, podcaster, author

"The most powerful books are born of an author's personal mining. I feel the mining in *Don't Miss Out* in every question Jeannie asks—every sentence laced with longing for more of the Holy Spirit. Don't miss out on this important book, indeed."

—Lisa Whittle, Bible teacher and bestselling
author of *Jesus Over Everything*

"Do you ever struggle to comprehend the person—and the role—of the Holy Spirit? Does He seem mystical, distant, or worse yet, even silent? When you read about the Spirit emboldening Christians on the pages of Scripture, do you wonder why you're not experiencing that same power today? Jeannie Cunnion's *Don't Miss Out* is a helpful resource that removes the mystery and unearths what is missing—a dynamic understanding and daily relationship with the third person of the Trinity. On its pages you will learn how the Holy Spirit, our promised Helper, can effectively empower you to live and love more like Jesus."

—Karen Ehman, *New York Times* bestselling
author and speaker

"I love this book! Jeannie Cunnion takes the sometimes confusing, often misunderstood, and almost always under-appreciated person of the Holy Spirit and brings Him into our lives in all His magnificent glory. Whether you're meeting Him for the first time or you've known God's Spirit for years, you'll discover irresistible power in these pages."

—Jodie Berndt, bestselling author of *Praying
the Scriptures for Your Children*

"*Don't Miss Out* isn't just a book—it's an eye-opening, soul-searching experience. Jeannie's heart to fully know and rely on the Holy Spirit is simply contagious. This is a must-read for those who are desperate to know all of God."

—Courtney DeFeo, author of *In This House,
We Will Giggle* and *Treasured*

"Jeannie's words have been forged in an authentic life. She's a woman who carries the Word through her experiences, and what we read from her pen is infused with Him. I'm grateful for her voice in these uncertain times."

—Sara Hagerty, bestselling author of *Adore* and *Unseen:
The Gift of Being Hidden in a World That Loves to Be Noticed*

"I was absolutely blown away, encouraged, and inspired by this book. In *Don't Miss Out*, my dear friend Jeannie Cunnion reminds us that where we 'can't,' GOD CAN! In every page, we are reminded to TAP IN to the incredible power of the Holy Spirit, who is available, who enables us to walk into the fullness of our calling.

For any who may feel 'stuck' in their walks with God, struggling with the same strongholds or lacking victory in areas, this book is a game changer. Jeannie tells of the beautiful gifts we have been given in getting FULL access to the precious Holy Spirit; may we receive and walk with Him today. This is a life-changing book!"

—Meshali Mitchell, photographer, podcast host
of *A Thousand Words*, and founder of *A House God Is Building*

"Jeannie is doing what few of us dare to do. She is taking God at His Word. Join Jeannie on her journey to make the Spirit as relevant and necessary to the Christian life as God promises. She shares her journey into God's presence and power with vulnerability and simplicity that will be sure to encourage you on yours."

—Jonathan Pitts, president, For Girls Like You Ministries

"Jeannie Cunnion takes the complex feast of 'Who is the Holy Spirit' and breaks it down into delicious bite-sized pieces. She writes in a way that distills deep theology into everyday vocabulary and helpful stories. Pick this one up; it will change you."

—Jessica Thompson, author/speaker

*don't
miss out*

don't miss out

DARING TO BELIEVE
LIFE IS BETTER
WITH THE HOLY SPIRIT

JEANNIE CUNNION

BETHANYHOUSE
a division of Baker Publishing Group
Minneapolis, Minnesota

© 2021 by Jeannie Cunnion

Published by Bethany House Publishers
11400 Hampshire Avenue South
Bloomington, Minnesota 55438
www.bethanyhouse.com

Bethany House Publishers is a division of
Baker Publishing Group, Grand Rapids, Michigan

Printed in the United States of America

Library of Congress Cataloging-in-Publication Data
Names: Cunnion, Jeannie, author.
Title: Don't miss out : daring to believe life is better with the Holy Spirit / Jeannie Cunnion.
Description: Minneapolis, Minnesota : Bethany House, a division of Baker Publishing Group, [2021]
Identifiers: LCCN 2020050779 | ISBN 9780764238222 (paper) | ISBN 9780764239069 (casebound) | ISBN 9781493431670 (ebook)
Subjects: LCSH: Holy Spirit.
Classification: LCC BT121.3 .C86 2021 | DDC 231/.3—dc23
LC record available at https://lccn.loc.gov/2020050779

The appendix, "Spiritual Gifts Survey," is from LifeWay Christian Resources Spiritual Gifts Survey. Copyright © 2003 LifeWay Christian Resources. Reprinted and used by permission.

Unless otherwise indicated, Scripture quotations are from The Holy Bible, English Standard Version® (ESV®), copyright © 2001 by Crossway, a publishing ministry of Good News Publishers. Used by permission. All rights reserved. ESV Text Edition: 2016

Scripture quotations identified GNT are from the Good News Translation in Today's English Version-Second Edition. Copyright © 1992 by American Bible Society. Used by permission.

Scripture quotations identified MESSAGE are from THE MESSAGE, copyright © 1993, 1994, 1995, 1996, 2000, 2001, 2002 by Eugene H. Peterson. Used by permission of NavPress. All rights reserved. Represented by Tyndale House Publishers, Inc.

Scripture quotations identified NIV are from the Holy Bible, New International Version®. NIV®. Copyright © 1973, 1978, 1984, 2011 by Biblica, Inc.™ Used by permission of Zondervan. All rights reserved worldwide. www.zondervan.com. The "NIV" and "New International Version" are trademarks registered in the United States Patent and Trademark Office by Biblica, Inc.™

Scripture quotations identified NLV are from the New Life Version. Copyright © 1969, 2003 by Barbour Publishing, Inc.

Scripture quotations identified NLT are from the *Holy Bible*, New Living Translation, copyright © 1996, 2004, 2007, 2013, 2015 by Tyndale House Foundation. Used by permission of Tyndale House Publishers, Inc., Carol Stream, Illinois 60188. All rights reserved.

Cover design by Emily Weigel
Cover artwork by Andrea Howey

Author is represented by Wolgemuth and Associates.

In keeping with biblical principles of creation stewardship, Baker Publishing Group advocates the responsible use of our natural resources. As a member of the Green Press Initiative, our company uses recycled paper when possible. The text paper of this book is composed in part of post-consumer waste.

green press INITIATIVE

21 22 23 24 25 26 27   7 6 5 4 3 2 1

This is dedicated to Andre and the children at
Danita's Children in Haiti.
Your precious lives bear witness to the hope
that overflows by the power of the Holy Spirit.
His presence in you gave me an insatiable thirst
to experience more of His presence in me!
Romans 15:13

Contents

Introduction

On a very ordinary day, I was invited to do an extraordinary thing. I signed the contract to write this book.

I'd asked my son Owen to get the mail for me, and when he came inside and dropped it on the counter, I noticed the manila envelope at the bottom of the stack, and I squealed. I knew the contract was coming, and I'd been eager to put my signature on the dotted line. It doesn't matter if it's your first or your fifteenth book contract, the gift of writing books that point to Jesus is something I will always celebrate. It's what I love to do, and I don't take the opportunity for granted.

Before Owen left the kitchen, I asked him to grab my phone and take a picture of me holding the contract. I wanted a photo to remember this special moment.

As Owen was positioning himself to take the photo from across the kitchen counter, Batman suddenly popped into the picture. Unbeknownst to me, my four-year-old son, Finn, had put on his Batman mask and was living his best life in the living room, but he'd come into the kitchen for a snack. And because he never misses a photo op, he asked, "Can I be in the picture, Mommy?"

I asked Owen to wait while I pulled up a stool so Batman could join me.

Owen took several pictures and handed the phone back to me. As I scrolled through the photos, the imagery wasn't lost on me. A superhero, with "supernatural ability," was with me. It felt like sweet assurance from Jesus that the Holy Spirit would guide me and give me wisdom as I wrote a book that I had fought writing. Yes, I fought this one hard.

In fact, if you'd told me even a year ago that I'd be writing a book about the Holy Spirit, I would have told you that you're precious but crazy. Only highly trained theologians with lots of letters after their name are qualified to write on the Spirit of God. And the topic is too divisive. And I have too much still to learn about the Holy Spirit's presence and power in my own life to be writing about how others can encounter and experience Him. Those are only three of the top ten reasons I offered to God in resistance to writing this book when He began disturbing me about the purpose of His Spirit. (And I mean disturbing in the best way.) But thankfully, God is persistent.

I want you to know I'm not writing this book as an expert who has sought to solve the mysteries of the Spirit, but as someone who stands in awe of the Three-In-One, and whose life has been (and continues to be) immensely bettered by growing in my relationship with the Spirit of God.

I also want you to know this book wasn't birthed from one big revelatory moment but from several small ones that, together, revealed something I absolutely didn't expect to discover: I've been settling for less than *all* of God by neglecting the supernatural power of the Spirit who lives in me.

But here's the thing: Neglecting the Holy Spirit wasn't an intentional decision. I simply didn't know very much about who He is, what He does, and why it matters so much. I think that's how it is for a lot of us. We just don't know.

Even though I have been following Jesus since I was eight years old, I know and believe the core doctrines of Christianity, and I had plenty of exposure to the Holy Spirit's work as a preacher's kid in an evangelical church, I didn't know all of the benefits I was missing out on by not being more reliant on the Spirit's presence and power in my life.

But God, in His infinite kindness, heard my daily prayers for a fuller knowledge and experience of His love in Jesus. And He answered that prayer by reintroducing me to His Spirit.

> I didn't know all of the benefits I was missing out on by not being more reliant on the Spirit's presence and power in my life.

Where It All Began

It all began about a year after my last book, *Mom Set Free*, was released. *Mom Set Free* is the story of how I was *finally* set free from the pressure to get it all right in my life and in my parenting, and I was set free to rest in God's sovereignty over my significance in my kids' lives. Ultimately, it's the story of how I learned to embrace and enjoy the freedom for which Christ has set us free as women and as moms.

But while I was busy speaking at conferences about our freedom in Christ, I began to struggle again at home with patterns and fears I'd been set free from. Yes, we are indeed forgetful people who never outgrow our need to hear the hope of the Gospel every single day, but it was more than that. What I ultimately realized through my struggles is that I was *set free* by Jesus, but I was trying to *live free* by Jeannie.

Around this same time, I was invited to speak to a lovely group of moms about relying on the Holy Spirit to accomplish His work in our kids' lives. When I finished speaking, we opened up the discussion for Q&A, and that was when one wise woman asked a significant question: "I know we are supposed to rely on the Holy Spirit, but how do we actually *do* that? How do we access

His power and teach it to our kids?" The truth is, I didn't have a very helpful answer for her, beyond explaining how Scripture tells us to ask for His help and to trust He will show up.

That's when I began to grapple with questions like,

Do I really *rely on the power of God's Spirit inside me, or am I mostly trying to do life in my own strength and supply?*
What do I really *know of Him?*
How can I experience more of His presence?
Why do I keep struggling with things I've been set free from?

In search of answers, I opened my Bible to study the Holy Spirit's work and, unsurprisingly, found Him in countless verses that I've read a hundred times but had failed to see Him at play in. I began to hear His name in worship songs I've sung a thousand times. I began to devour books about the Holy Spirit by theologians and teachers I respect.

Through my searching and learning, I began to see how I'd treated the Holy Spirit as though He were the optional part of the Trinity. As though God asks, "Would you like the Holy Spirit too?" when we put our trust in Jesus, just as a server at a restaurant asks, "Would you like ketchup too?" when we order fries. This discovery stirred in me a fear of missing out, but this wasn't your typical fear of missing out—or what we call FOMO. It was a holy FOMO. I had *holy fear* that I was settling for less than *all* of God.

You should also know that as I studied and welcomed the Spirit to get in my business, I quickly realized that writing this book was going to hurt a bit. It became clear I had not fully surrendered areas in my life that the Spirit wanted full access to. (I'll be telling you all about those areas in the pages to come. We're going to get very honest here.) Yes, I knew that writing this book would come at a cost, but the more I learned about the beautiful person of the Holy Spirit and the more I got to know Him as my friend, the more I craved His presence and the more I knew I needed His power.

16

What became undeniable was that I was functioning mostly in my own power. I was trying to grow and bloom and love and witness in my own power rather than in the Spirit's power. All the while, God was inviting me into the *super-over-natural* life.

He wanted to infuse His super into my natural. That's what He wants to do in all of us!

Saying yes to God's invitation profoundly changed me and propelled me to write the book I'd been fighting, because it was too good to keep to myself. The Holy Spirit is so much better and so much bigger than I ever imagined.

I want each one of us to know this in our bones: Jesus' life set us free and the Spirit's power *keeps* us free! Free from settling for less than all that God wants to do in us and for us and through us. I am desperate for each one of us to love Him and welcome His supernatural work in our lives because He wants to draw us deeper into the life-giving, soul-satisfying, and utterly transforming love of Jesus, for the glory of the Father.

> Jesus' life set us free and the Spirit's power *keeps* us free!

What *Doesn't* the Holy Spirit Do?

I also want you to know I am not attempting to answer all of our questions about the Holy Spirit in this book. The Holy Spirit is as mysterious as He is made-known, and questions will remain around the more complex conversations we could (but won't) have about the Holy Spirit. This is not an extensive theological treatise about the Holy Spirit but a personal invitation to better know and experience Him. This is not a comprehensive book, but an intimate look at His inexhaustive and incomparable role in our lives.

There are so many strong (and often divisive) opinions around the Holy Spirit that distract us and make Him seem not only confusing but intimidating, leading most of us to just dismiss Him because He seems to be the hardest of the Trinity to grasp. What we tend to overlook is that there are things about the Holy Spirit that are made wonderfully and beautifully clear in Scripture, and that is where I will steer us in these pages. And while it is utterly impossible to encapsulate the third person of the Trinity, I do believe we will—with every turn of the page—feel like we're getting to know better the friend above every other friend.

The extent to which we are willing to engage with the Spirit of God is the extent to which we will encounter the fullness of God. So, if you are willing to get really honest with yourself—and with God—about those things that are keeping you from enjoying His indwelling presence, experiencing His power, and exercising the gifts He's given you, you can't imagine what's coming! It won't always be easy (because few things worth having are), but it will be *so* worth it.

> The extent to which we are willing to engage with the Spirit of God is the extent to which we will encounter the fullness of God.

My hope is that, at the end of this journey, our main question will no longer be, "What does the Holy Spirit do?" but rather, "What *doesn't* the Holy Spirit do?" because He is working in so many ways that I don't think most of us even realize or take advantage of. He has so much to show us and to do in us and through us!

Oh, and here's the other thing I trust will happen in you, because it's happened in me, and it's a precious gift. Through this journey, God has been showing me where I have, all along, been experiencing His power and provision and presence in ways I simply didn't notice before. I've seen where He has been empowering me, molding me, convicting and comforting me, guiding and growing me, in ways I would have missed had I not accepted God's call to write this book for *us*. It gave me a deep sense of gratitude for how He's been working even when I didn't see it. (Isn't that crazy, though? God doesn't pout and pull back when we aren't mindful of or grateful for His goodness. He patiently waits for us to be astonished by Him.)

But I don't want to miss it anymore. I don't want to overlook His presence and fail to celebrate His provision. I'm here for it! And that is why I finally stopped giving God all my excuses about being unworthy of writing a book about His Spirit.

I wrote this book, which I hope feels more like an invitation from a close friend, with the hope that none of us will miss out on experiencing the benefits of the **last-to-be-mentioned but not least-in-significance** person of the Trinity, the greatest benefit being hearts enlarged for Jesus. That is the Holy Spirit's priority, after all—to make much of Jesus!

Last but Not Least

At the end of each chapter you will find a "Last but Not Least" simple exercise to help you connect with the benefit of the Holy Spirit that was revealed in that chapter. "Last but Not Least" is meant to remind us that though the Holy Spirit is named last when we speak of the Trinity, it does not follow that He is least in significance. I kept the chapters shorter in length so we can pause at the end of each one to reflect on the benefit God wants us to experience through His Spirit. You can also download discussion questions for your group or book club at JeannieCunnion.com.

As personally as I can say this, I want you to know how happy I am that you are holding this book in your hands, because I believe the Three-In-One is about to blow us away.

one

He Is to Our Advantage

Much of my relationship with the Holy Spirit has been like the simultaneous gesturing we do using one hand to wave someone toward us with a "Come closer" motion while holding up our other hand at the end of our outstretched arm signaling "Stop right there." Yes, it's fair to say my posture with the Spirit of God was one of hesitation more than cooperation.

I can't help but wonder what words you would use to describe your feelings about or experience with the Holy Spirit.

In conversations with Christian friends from varying walks of life, I've asked what words they would use to describe their feelings about the Holy Spirit. A few shared how He was crucial to their faith and how they felt very connected to Him, but by and large, most friends expressed feelings of uncertainty or disconnection.

Our uncertainty about the Holy Spirit isn't surprising, considering the way the He has been misused and misunderstood in the church and in culture. Most Christians are comfortable with God the Father and God the Son, but we assume that God the Spirit is reserved for the extremes: either the super-spiritual or the super-strange.

The stigma is that if you speak freely of the Holy Spirit, you must be a very religious person who got so close to God that you got access to His Spirit, or you must be one of those slightly off people who behaves a bit dramatically while doing sensational things in the name of the Holy Spirit.

Because of this stigma, most Christians casually recite the seven words we often find in Scripture—"through the power of the Holy Spirit"—but rarely do we actually know what that means or welcome His transforming power in our lives. We settle for less than *all* of God. Let me make that more personal. *I* settled for less than all of God.

Have We Settled?

The irony is, if you had asked me to describe my faith life a couple years ago, I never would have thought to use the word *settling*, because I love my King Jesus and I know how desperately I need His mercy and grace. He is the lover of my soul. But as I began to awaken to the Holy Spirit's presence and power inside me, what I discovered stunned me, because settling is—in many ways— exactly what I'd been doing by not relying more on the Holy Spirit's supernatural presence, provision, and power dwelling in me.

> I was settling for far less than all that God offers us.

It's not that I didn't believe in and affirm the Trinity—God the Father, God the Son, and God the Holy Spirit. I wholeheartedly did. I was just neglecting the extraordinary benefits of the indwelling presence of God's Spirit. This discovery lit a fire in me because it revealed I was settling for far less than all that God offers us.

In fact, I vividly remember several mornings of sitting in my office chair, my Bible open on my desk and a very large hot coffee in my hand, reading chapters 14 through 16 in the gospel of John specifically in search of the Holy Spirit's presence on the pages, being utterly awestruck at what I've missed. The question that kept running through my mind was, *How have I been following Jesus since I was eight years old, faithfully attending church, and reading Scripture and attending more Bible studies than I can count, but somehow neglecting the very One Jesus said is to my advantage?*

Did you know that about the Holy Spirit? Did you know that Jesus said He is to your advantage? Read these words of Jesus slowly:

> But now I am going to him who sent me, and none of you asks me, "Where are you going?" But because I have said these things to you, sorrow has filled your heart. Nevertheless, I tell you the truth: it is to your advantage that I go away, for if I do not go away, the Helper will not come to you. But if I go, I will send him to you.
>
> John 16:5–7

The "Helper" Jesus is speaking about in verse 7 is, of course, the Holy Spirit. Jesus knows His disciples are deeply disappointed that His departure is imminent, so He lovingly assures them, "Trust me on this! It is *better* that I return to my Father *so that* the Holy Spirit will come" (my paraphrase). Other translations read "it is better for you," "for your good," and "for your benefit." Isn't it so interesting that Jesus didn't say it was "almost as good" or even "just as good" for them to have His Spirit *in them* rather than His physical presences *with them*. He said it was "better," and it was only going to happen if He ascended to His Father.

The twelve disciples weren't disappointed because they didn't want the Holy Spirit. They were disappointed because it meant Jesus was going to depart. This was devastating news for the men who'd just spent three years by His side and under His leadership. I'm guessing their sadness was also anchored in their inability to even begin to fathom what they would soon gain in the Helper.

23

It is no small thing that Jesus' revelation to His disciples remains true for us more than two thousand years later. And yet, we might be tempted to respond to this news as the disciples did. "Better for us that you leave? No. How could it be better? How could anything be better than you right here beside us? We want *you*, Jesus, not just the Helper, your Spirit."

I can't help but wonder what Jesus would say to those of us feeling unsure, even now, about it being better to have His Spirit living in us over His physical presence beside us. I envision Jesus responding with tenderness, yet certainty, saying something like:

"But daughter, God the Father, God the Son, and God the Holy Spirit are One. The Holy Spirit makes me even more real and beautiful to you. He takes up residence in your heart so you will never be alone and never be without what you need. He is making you more like me. And let me tell you what else He can do for you. Oh, just let me tell you how He is to your advantage!"

How the Holy Spirit is to our advantage, and all the benefits we enjoy by receiving His indwelling presence, is what we are about to discover together. And it's going to be so good!

How Is the Spirit to Our Advantage?

Jesus was "God with us." The Holy Spirit is "God in us."

See, the disciples thought they were losing closeness and connectivity with Jesus, when really He would be closer and more connected to them than ever before because His Spirit would now take up residence inside them. And that same closeness and connectivity is accessible to us today, through His Spirit!

Even more than that, knowing we have the Holy Spirit living inside us should give us extraordinary confidence. What is more empowering than knowing Almighty God indwells us?

When facing a frightening diagnosis, navigating financial hardship or crisis, fighting fear over an uncertain future, praying to better love a difficult spouse, feeling hopeless over foolish choices our children are making, or struggling with the same old sins and strongholds, we can stand confidently on the power of the Holy Spirit, who is our divine Helper. This is not flimsy or false confidence. This is certified confidence. He is more than able!

I need you to know that whatever lies before you, it's not all on you! It's on the Spirit *in* you. And if His power can raise our Savior from the grave, He can handle whatever hardship or fear you face.

But there's more.

The Spirit gives us confidence that we can live out the call of the Gospel because He supplies the ability. We don't have to muster up heart motivation to worship God above all our other loves. The Spirit does that *in* us. And then He gives us the boldness to spread the Gospel to a world desperately in need of healing and hope.

This is all the work of the Spirit. This is why Jesus said it's to our advantage that the Holy Spirit comes. His work in our lives is so connected and crucial to experiencing the fullness of God.

> His work in our lives is so connected and crucial to experiencing the fullness of God.

The Holy Spirit, our consummate Helper, guides us, comforts us, fills us with hope and joy, gives us life and peace, strengthens us in our inner being, communicates with us, prays for us, leads us in truth, empowers us to fight sin, illuminates Scripture, and advocates for us. He opens our hearts to the love of Jesus, makes us more like Jesus, and gives us supernatural gifts to build up the church and glorify God.

This, and so much more, is what we will unpack thoroughly in the chapters to come, as we discover how Jesus' ascension ushered in a new depth and dimension in our relationship with God. This is worthy of celebration.

I believe that the deeper we dig into Scripture, and the more we open ourselves up to experiencing the Spirit's presence and power in our daily doings, the more we'll find ourselves grateful that Christ ascended and the Holy Spirit descended. We'll discover Jesus was right all along. Why do we ever doubt?

Oh, how I want us to know Him and enjoy the benefits of being filled by Him. This is an invitation to discover how essential the Holy Spirit is to the full and flourishing Christian life. He can do more in you and through you than you ever thought possible. (And if you haven't put your trust in Jesus, please keep reading, as this is every bit as much for you! The very fact that you're holding this book in your hand tells me God is in passionate pursuit of you, patiently waiting for you to say yes to Jesus and receive His Spirit!)

It's time to stop settling for mere knowledge of His existence and start enjoying the many benefits of His presence.

last but not least

Reflect: Why is it difficult to believe that it is to our advantage to have His Spirit living *in* us over having His physical presence *beside* us?

Respond: Today, adopt a conscious awareness of God's Spirit in you. Have you felt comforted? Been empowered to do the right thing in a difficult situation? Used a spiritual gift to bless the life of another? Read a verse that suddenly made more sense than ever before? Friend, that's the Holy Spirit . . . *in you!*

two

He Makes His Home in Us

The Holy Spirit stirred my heart to repentance the night my mom took me to see the Billy Graham movie *The Prodigal* at a theater in Deerfield Beach, Florida. My motivation for going to the movie with my mom wasn't receiving salvation. It was getting a bag of Twizzlers and a soda. But my heart was so convicted by the Spirit in that theater that when we got home, I crawled into bed, overwhelmed with certainty of my need for Jesus. I remember the moment my mom walked into the bedroom to find me under the covers. When she leaned down to kiss me good-night, I asked her to pray with me. I told her I wanted to put my trust in Jesus and accept Him as my Savior.

Since that moment, I have lived in the confidence that I am saved from condemnation for my sins, and that I am freely given abundant and eternal life in Christ. This is a gift that can't be earned by anything I do, and it certainly isn't deserved, and there is absolutely nothing I can do to add to, or subtract from, the work of Christ on my behalf. It's all grace. This is the salvation narrative—the Good News that changed my life.

What has struck me recently, however, is how the salvation narrative doesn't typically include the gift we are given in the indwelling Holy Spirit. Why is it that when we share the good news of the Gospel—and how it means we are forgiven and secure for eternity—we don't tend to also talk about the priceless treasure deposited inside us to live a free and full life infused with the power of God's Spirit in the present?

How I wish I'd heard more about the Spirit's power for our daily life in my earlier years of following of Jesus. Or maybe I did hear it but I just wasn't listening. I only recall being familiar with the conversations (and divisions) around the gifts of the Spirit, and I think He got stuck in the "spiritual gifts" box. This is why I long to see Him woven more into our narrative, because there is no part of the Christian life that isn't utterly dependent of the Spirit's power *in us*. It's the "in us" that gets me. When we put our trust in Jesus, God puts His Spirit in us! It's an extravagant exchange, all to our advantage and all for God's glory.

Paul writes, "He redeemed us in order that the blessing given to Abraham might come to the Gentiles through Christ Jesus, so that by faith we might receive the promise of the Spirit" (Galatians 3:14 NIV).

See, salvation is a gift we receive—not earn—when we repent and follow Jesus. *Likewise*, the Holy Spirit is a gift we receive—not earn—when we repent and follow Jesus.[1]

How wild to think that belief in Jesus is the only prerequisite to receiving the powerful Holy Spirit inside us. This should stun us. And yet, I think a lot of us believe that having a Spirit-filled life looks more like a ladder to climb. We might think it looks something like this:

Rung 1—You receive salvation.
Rung 2—Maybe you get some sort of access to His Spirit.
Rung 3—Maybe you get some measure of His supernatural power.

Rung 4—Maybe you get spiritual gifts, but maybe that's just for other Christians.

Rung 5—Maybe you get the "higher gifts."[2]

But this couldn't be further from the truth. The Holy Spirit is not Someone we earn *access* to at some point in our walk with Christ once we attain a certain level of knowledge or holiness. If you are a follower of Jesus, He is *in* you, He is *for* you, and He is for *now*. By faith alone we receive the Spirit, just as God promised.

He Is God's Personal Presence Inside Us

In John chapters 14 through 16, Jesus promises the ministry of the Holy Spirit to His disciples and details much of what the Spirit will do for them. I can't wait for us to dive into all the details of these chapters. For now, though, I want to highlight two glorious takeaways from John 14:16–17 (emphasis added). Let's read it together. Jesus said,

> And I will ask the Father, and he will give you another Helper to be with you forever, even the Spirit of truth, whom the world cannot receive, because it neither sees him nor knows him. You know him, for he dwells with you and *will be in you.*

The first glorious truth being revealed here is found in Jesus promising an unfathomable bond between us and the Holy Spirit when He said (my paraphrase), "My Father will give you another Helper . . . who will not only be *with* you but will live *in* you!"

Let's do a quick glance back in history to see the significance of this statement.

"The operations of the Holy Spirit among men in the three periods of human history may be defined by three words: 'upon,' 'with,' and 'in.' In the Old Testament He came *upon* selected persons and remained for a season (Judges 14:19). In the Gospels

He is represented as dwelling *with* the disciples in the person of Christ (John 14:17). From the second chapter of Acts onward He is spoken of as being *in* the people of God (1 Corinthians 6:19)," wrote Billy Graham.[3]

Living *in* the people of God was an entirely new phenomenon because previous to Pentecost, the Holy Spirit primarily resided upon people or with people. But now Jesus was promising something so much greater. He said that though the disciples already knew the Holy Spirit because He was *with* them, now He would live *in* them. And it would have nothing to do with their behavior or theology or good works. It would have everything to do with grace. Jesus knew the Holy Spirit was about to indwell ordinary— and often fearful—people to transform them with His supernatural power.

The Holy Spirit is God's personal presence inside us. Does this blow our minds? I mean, seriously, what kind of God chooses to indwell His people? Our God! He is unfathomably good.

He Exists to Help Us!

The next glorious truth being revealed here is the kind of helper the Holy Spirit will be.

The Greek word translated "helper" in this verse is *parakletos*— which literally means "called to one's side."[4] But this wasn't just any helper. See, even more exciting is how Jesus said the Holy Spirit would be "*another* Helper." The Greek word translated "another" in this verse is *allon*—which, in this context, translates as "another of the same kind."[5]

So Jesus is assuring the disciples, and us, that the Holy Spirit isn't "less than" Him or even "similar" to Him, but just like Him!

How are they different but the same? That's a good and complicated question, so I defer to the brilliant mind of Tim Keller for the explanation. He writes, "Many people say that the Holy Spirit gives us power, and that's true, but how does He do that?

Does He merely zap us with higher energy levels? No—by calling him the *other* Advocate [or Helper], Jesus has given us the great clue to understanding how the empowering of the Holy Spirit works. The first advocate [Jesus] is speaking to God for you, but the second Advocate [the Holy Spirit] is speaking to *you* for you."[6]

The Holy Spirit is speaking *to* you, *for* you. Do you know all the ways He is for you and wants to help you? Check this out.

In the ESV translation, we just read the Holy Spirit is called "another Helper" by Jesus, but in other translations—because *parakletos* is too full of meaning to translate into just one word— the Holy Spirit is also called our "Comforter," "Counselor," "Advocate," "Strengthener," "Intercessor," "Standby," and "Champion." Maybe read that list again. Slowly. Let it sink in.

What will make a dramatic *difference* in how you live is knowing that God Almighty dwells inside you by His Spirit, and then believing that everything that is His is yours. His power. His wisdom. His strength and joy. His peace and comfort. His love. God manifests *all* of himself, in His people, through His Spirit.

> Everything we need is inside of us—all and only—because the Holy Spirit inside us is all-sufficient.

If you're struggling to love an unlovable person, or forgive an offense that the world tells you is unforgivable, or heal from a devastating heartbreak, the Holy Spirit wants to help you. He is *able* to help you. How do we know? Because the Holy Spirit's role is to make us more like Jesus, and this is who Jesus is. He loves His enemies, forgives His accusers and killers, and brings wholeness and healing to brokenness.

Where there are strongholds of sin that need to be broken. Where there is spiritual warfare that needs to be won. Where there is toxic thinking that needs breakthrough. This is where the Spirit of God is desperately needed and more than capable.

Do we believe this? Everything we need is inside of us—all and only—because the Holy Spirit inside us is all-sufficient. He lacks nothing and He holds nothing back from His children.

This doesn't mean we don't need community or friendship or help from outside sources. It means we can have confidence because the God inside us wholly equips us for what's before us.

He Transforms Us

The Spirit of God indwells every believer for a very specific purpose. To help us! He helps us live out our salvation in the supernatural power of God and grow in the likeness of Jesus, the One who rescued us.

I think one of the biggest obstacles to us having "life to the fullest"—as Jesus promised us in John 10:10—is believing that once we accept Christ as our Savior, it's *our* job to grow in holiness. We might believe it's our job to fight bad habits and sin, and it's our job to make our lives look more like His. Of course, we have a very important role to play in growing in Christlikeness. We have to submit to and cooperate with the Spirit!

But no growth can be accomplished in our own power. Operating in our own power will only produce temporary behavior change and natural results, but the Holy Spirit works from the inside out. He changes the desires and motives of our heart. He doesn't just do touch-ups. He transforms us. He does the supernatural.

> He doesn't just do touch-ups. He transforms us. He does the supernatural.

No wonder there are so many Jesus dropouts. No wonder so many will say, "I tried following Jesus, but no matter how hard I tried, I felt like I couldn't be good enough, so I just quit trying." None of us can follow Jesus without the power of the Holy Spirit. We need the Spirit's indwelling help!

Do You Have the Holy Spirit?

D. Martyn Lloyd-Jones said it so well: "Those who have received the Holy Spirit are aware of a power dealing with them and working in them. A disturbance, something, someone interfering in our lives. We are going along, and suddenly we are arrested and pulled up, and we find ourselves different. That is the beginning; that is what always happens when the Holy Ghost begins to work in a human being. There is a disturbance, an interruption to the normal ordinary tenor of life. There is something different, an awareness of being dealt with—I cannot put it better; that is the essence of the Holy Spirit dealing with us."[7]

But here's something else we need to know. Though the Holy Spirit is a gift to all who believe, not everyone enjoys the gift. I don't want any of us to look back on our lives and have to say, "Oh, how I wish I had known about the gift of the Holy Spirit's transforming power in my life. I wish I'd heeded the interruptions! I wish I'd known all the benefits that were mine in the One Jesus said was to my advantage." And while I don't think any of us will ever fully grasp all He does in us and for us, we'd be foolish not to seek it! Because even though all Christians are indwelt by the Holy Spirit, not all Christians are living in the power of the Spirit.

> Though the Holy Spirit is a gift to all who believe, not everyone enjoys the gift.

If you have put your faith in Jesus, then rest assured, at this very moment, the Holy Spirit lives inside you. He is the best friend you will ever have. He is eager to give you everything you need to pursue the person of Christ, grow in the perfection of Christ, and spread the Gospel of Christ. He wants to awaken you to His transforming power inside you. He wants to make Jesus more beautiful to you!

last but not least

Reflect: Read Acts 2:38. Fill in the blank. "Repent and be baptized, every one of you, in the name of Jesus Christ for the forgiveness of your sins. And you _____ _____ the gift of the Holy Spirit." Based on the words you wrote in the blanks provided, how certain is the gift of the Holy Spirit in the life of a confessed believer?

Respond: If you have already put your trust in Jesus, take a moment right now to thank Him for choosing to put His very Spirit in you, and ask Him to grow your gratitude for this extraordinary gift!

And if you haven't put your trust in Jesus, and you sense Him wooing your heart to His through the conviction of the Holy Spirit, welcome His life-changing love right where you are. You don't have to speak some magic set of words. It's as simple for you as it was for me when I told my mom that I wanted to put my trust in Jesus. Repent of your sin, confess Him as God's only Son, and receive the gift of everlasting life and the indwelling presence of God's Spirit.

three

He Never Leaves Us

My youngest son, Finn, loves Dr. Seuss books. One of his favorites is the classic *Oh, the Places You'll Go!* We've read it countless times, but on one recent evening, a particular line in the book jumped out at me and bothered me enough that before I turned the page to keep reading, I reworded the sentence to change the message, and then I read the page to Finn again in my own words. Every word matters.

The sentence read, "*All alone!* Whether you like it or not, Alone will be something you'll be quite a lot."[1] But now when we get to that page, I substitute, "All alone is something we will never be because the Holy Spirit lives inside you and me." Not too shabby, right? I want Finn to know, even at four years old, that he will never be alone because God's Spirit will never leave him.

We know the Holy Spirit indwells us, but just as miraculous is this: He never abandons us. One of the most precious things about the Holy Spirit is that we never have to fear His abandonment. Even in our loneliest moments, we are never truly alone. Even on our most rebellious days, He stays. And here's the other thing: He helps *us* stay. When the day feels too hard to face and we want to quit showing up, or when we want to run from relationships or make ourselves numb to our hard realities, He helps us stay, because He stays too. And there isn't anything we can't face when we know we have the power of the Spirit inside us.

The Holy Spirit is the most loyal companion we will ever have. Oh, we can grieve Him and we can quench Him, but we cannot lose Him. This is our remarkable post-Pentecost promise, but it wasn't always this way. Let's talk about that.

Our Post-Pentecost Promise

In the Old Testament, the Holy Spirit came *upon* people to equip and empower them for a specific work, but they could not count on His presence as permanent.

For example, when Samuel anointed Saul as the first king of Israel, 1 Samuel 10:10 (NIV) says "the Spirit of God came powerfully upon him, and he joined in their prophesying." The power of the Spirit was so apparent in Saul's life then, but later in his reign, when Saul chose not to obey God fully during the attack on the Amalekites—he spared the Amalekite king and he got greedy and kept some of the loot God told him to destroy—God removed the Holy Spirit from him and everything went south from there.[2] Without the presence and power of the Holy Spirit, Saul could not successfully serve as king, and he ultimately died in battle.

When God removed His Spirit from Saul, He chose David as the second king of Israel. "So Samuel took the horn of oil and anointed him in the presence of his brothers, and from that day on the Spirit of the LORD came powerfully upon David" (1 Samuel 16:13 NIV).

Here is the word *upon* again, and it matters greatly. See, as you likely know, David has a remarkable story, having been called the ideal king. From slaying Goliath to taking the ark of the covenant into Jerusalem, David served God faithfully in the power of Spirit, but like we are, David was fallible, as is most clearly seen in his story with Bathsheba.

David penned much of the Psalms, and he did so under the inspiration of the Holy Spirit, as is true of all writers of Scripture, but there is one particular passage that once troubled me greatly because I didn't understand then what I understand now.

Don't Take Your Spirit from Me

The passage I'm referring to is Psalm 51:1–19, where we read David's deeply remorseful and repentant prayer of confession after he is confronted by Nathan about his adultery with Bathsheba and the murder of her husband that he orchestrated.

This prayer is so powerful I'd encourage you to pause and read it in its entirety, but here I want to highlight where David begs God not to take His Spirit from him. David had seen, after all, how poorly things went for Saul when God removed His Spirit from him.

David pleads, "Create in me a pure heart, O God, and renew a steadfast spirit within me. Do not cast me from your presence or take your Holy Spirit from me. Restore to me the joy of your salvation and grant me a willing spirit, to sustain me" (vv. 10–12 NIV).

In the Old Testament, when the Spirit came upon people for a purpose but not into them with His permanent presence, God could have taken the Holy Spirit from David as He did from Saul. But He didn't. He was merciful in David's humble confession and repentance, and let His Spirit remain.

Allowing His Spirit to remain on David doesn't mean God protected him from the very painful consequences of his sin, but He did not remove His Spirit from him. Like David, we will usually suffer the consequence of our sin, but unlike David, we never have to fear the ultimate consequence of losing the presence of God's Spirit.

When the weight of my sin and rebellion is heavy, David's prayer has put words to the ache in my heart and brought the certainty of cleansing and comfort. It assures me God will never remove His Spirit from me.

I Will Not Leave You as Orphans

A profound promise Jesus made to His disciples before His ascension was that the Holy Spirit would be with them "forever" and that He would not "leave them as orphans" (John 14:16–18).

As we know, an orphan is someone who has been permanently abandoned by their earthly parents, whether by death or by decision. Our son Andre, who joined our family in 2019 at the age of twenty-two, was an orphan in Haiti. His mom passed when he was three, and his dad placed him with Danita's Children's Home (a loving Christian orphanage) when Andre was seven, due to dire circumstances in the country. Soon thereafter, his dad also passed, so Andre remained at Danita's and grew up with about a hundred other children.

Andre was loved, nurtured, educated, and called *son* by the incredible missionaries at Danita's. Still, he knows the deep heartbreak of being orphaned. And even though most of us haven't endured what Andre did, most of us know the sting of abandonment in human relationships and the ensuing feelings of loneliness.

But the precious promise Jesus made to His disciples, and to us, is that we never have to fear being abandoned by Him because He gives us His permanent presence in the person of the Holy Spirit. We are never at risk of being left behind. We are never, ever, truly alone.

The New Epidemic

Did you know that loneliness is being called the new epidemic in America? Nearly half of Americans say they always or sometimes feel alone, and Gen Z has unsurprisingly been found to be the loneliest generation.[3]

Loneliness is actually the number one fear of young people today. They are more afraid of loneliness than they are of losing a home or a job, and 42 percent of millennial women are more afraid of loneliness than a cancer diagnosis. Scientists now recognize that loneliness not only leads to depression, anxiety, and other painful psychiatric disorders, but it also wreaks havoc on our bodies, leading to serious physical ailments.[4]

We've never needed to know the permanent and personal presence of our loyal friend, the Holy Spirit, like we do now. We need to know that He is still closer than our breath—even when it feels like God has ceased to uphold His promise to never abandon us because the pain runs so deep and the silence feels so deafening and life feels so disappointing. We need to know that He remains in us and for us.

I experienced the sting of abandonment and loneliness when I was walking through a deeply painful divorce. Living in my sister's basement bedroom and trying to put my life back together at twenty-five years old, I attempted to find solace in cheap bottles of red wine and a concerted effort to build a better life. But nothing could cure the bitter loneliness that iced a cake made with the ingredients of shame, rejection, and unlovability. It was brutal. I was ashamed of my inability to save the marriage and I was afraid God was irrevocably disappointed in me. Though surrounded by family and friends who loved me and committed to walking with me through that season, the undoing of two who became one was a pain I was not prepared for.

But this is what I didn't see then but I see so clearly now—the Holy Spirit was so very present with me. He was comforting me, advocating for me, and holding me together. I could have gone much deeper into misery. I could have completely self-destructed in an attempt to prove my false theory that God was right in rendering my life a useless testimony because of my failure.

Instead, the Holy Spirit was tenderly lifting my head to behold the grace of God in Jesus Christ. He was working overtime to

The Holy Spirit's ability to comfort us isn't confined to our awareness of His presence.

keep me from believing the lie that God was finished with me. He was giving me boldness to go before the throne of God, even with my cheap wine hangover, to wrap myself in the embrace of God. He was leading me into a radical new awareness and experience of God's grace. A grace that does its best work in our deepest pits.

While the feeling of loneliness consumed me, I believe my soul knew I was never really alone, even though my mind didn't comprehend it. Thankfully, the Holy Spirit's ability to comfort us isn't confined to our awareness of His presence. My heart is flooded with gratitude too big to articulate when I look back on how His presence was pervasive in that basement bedroom.

His Comfort in Our Suffering

I have known His daily comfort beyond the walls of my sister's basement. He has been comforting me during the days that just seem to go terribly awry and when life feels too big. And I have known His incomparable comfort in other deep losses, such as my miscarriage, as I said good-bye to the baby I won't hold till heaven. Yes, I felt His tender, warm presence enveloping me in that cold, sterile hospital room.

His comfort is the assurance that Jesus knows my pain, enters into my pain, and won't waste my pain. His comfort provides supernatural hope. Not the kind of hope like when we say, "I hope this thing happens" or "I hope I can heal from this pain." It is the hope of salvation that "will not lead to disappointment. For we know how dearly God loves us, because he has given us the Holy Spirit to fill our hearts with his love" (Romans 5:5 NLT).

His Spirit is more proof of how much He loves us. It's evidence of how much He values us. You don't put your very Spirit in something that isn't immensely precious to you. And through the power of His Spirit in us, we can have more than just a hopeful outlook in our suffering. We can supernaturally abound and prosper in hope (Romans 15:13).

I might not know what valleys you're walking through—or have come through—but I do know this: There are no circumstances that can cause the Holy Spirit to leave you behind. He doesn't give up on you when you give up on yourself. The Holy Spirit does not abandon you when you stumble into sin. Your sadness doesn't scare Him away! His abiding presence is internal *and* eternal. He is the faithful friend you long for, taking your hand and leading you toward your hope of wholeness.

last but not least

Reflect: Read Psalm 139:7. Based on this reading, where can you go to flee from God's Spirit?

Respond: Does that make you feel comforted or uncomfortable? Speak honestly to God about how you feel. Ask Him to heighten your awareness of His loyal companionship in your life.

four

He Is God

Years ago, when my son Brennan was around seven years old, he had a "revelation" about the Holy Spirit. This followed a conversation we had about how God gave us His Spirit to help us make good choices. A few hours after our talk, Brennan returned to very proudly tell me he'd figured out who the Holy Spirit is: "God is the Father. Jesus is the Son. And the Holy Spirit is the baby!"

We obviously still had some work to do with our young son around his theology, but I loved that he was trying to figure out who the Holy Spirit is! Maybe you can relate?

Of course, none of us would suggest that the Holy Spirit is the baby of the Trinity, but it's not unusual to have misconceptions about who the Holy Spirit *really* is, what He *really* does, and why that matters so much.

In exploring these things, we'll begin by acknowledging that our finite minds cannot completely comprehend our infinite God. We can echo the words of Isaiah: "Who can fathom the Spirit of the LORD, or instruct the LORD as his counselor?" (40:13 NIV). And still, the incomprehensible, mysterious, beautiful, trinitarian nature of God is what we will seek to better understand as we unpack Scripture, where many things are very much made known to us.

So if the Holy Spirit is not the baby of the Trinity, who is He? The Holy Spirit is God. God eternally exists as three persons: Father, Son, and Holy Spirit. There is one God, and each person in the Trinity is *fully* God.

Make sense? Of course! Kinda. Not really. Not yet. All of those answers are okay.

One of the most helpful ways I've learned to think about the complexity of the Three-In-One is through Billy Graham's explanation that "It is not one plus one plus one equals three. It is one times one times one equals one."[1]

From Genesis to Revelation

God the Father, God the Son, and God the Spirit coexist as the eternal (no beginning and no end), omnipresent (existing everywhere at all times), omniscient (knowing everything), omnipotent (all-powerful) Godhead.

"There is nothing God does not know; that's His omniscience. There is no place where He does not exist; that's His omnipresence. But that's not all. There is nothing God cannot do; that's His omnipotence," writes Tony Evans.[2] All these attributes belong to God the Father, God the Son, *and* God the Holy Spirit.

The first sentence in the Bible showcases their Godhead:

> In the beginning, God created the heavens and the earth. The earth was without form and void, and darkness was over the face of the deep. And the Spirit of God was hovering over the face of the waters.
>
> Genesis 1:1–2

In verse 1, the Hebrew word translated "God" is *Elohim*, and it is plural in form. This signifies that God the Father, God the Son, and God the Holy Spirit were working together in perfect harmony in creation. And in verse 2 we read explicitly that the

Spirit of God was hovering over the waters. Can you picture it? How beautiful and beyond comprehension this must have been! "Then God said, 'Let us make man in our image, after our likeness'" (Genesis 1:26). He didn't say "Let 'me' make man in 'my' likeness." The "us" and "our" demonstrate their tri-unity from before time began.

His Distinct Purpose

Throughout our study of Scripture, we will see the trinitarian nature of God on full display—or in what Richard Rohr so beautifully describes as the "divine dance"—but it's worth noting that we'll see how visibility of their unique functions will vary. Meaning, we will see how the work of the Father is most visible in the Old Testament, the work of the Son is most visible in the Gospels, and the work of the Holy Spirit is most visible from the Day of Pentecost to Revelation. However, the visibility of their unique functions is always intended to lead us to the fullness of the Godhead.

But when their different functions start to feel confusing and I get caught up in who does what, it helps me to remember that they are not competing with each other for my attention and they are not fighting for priority in my life. "There is no jealousy or rivalry in the Trinity," writes R. T. Kendall.[3]

The Spirit's presence is the manifestation of the Trinity among us today, and though He carries the same authority and shares the same attributes as God the Father and God the Son, He performs distinct functions. This is important and speaks to the tragedy of the Spirit often being neglected and forgotten. God the Holy Spirit does specific work in us that differs from that of God the Father and God the Son.

J. I. Packer puts it this way: "The Christian's life in all its aspects—intellectual and ethical, devotional and relational, upsurging in worship and outgoing in witness, is supernatural; only the Spirit can initiate it and sustain it. So apart from Him, not only will there be no lively believers and no lively congregations, there will be no believers and no congregations at all."[4]

Do we believe that? Do we believe that God the Holy Spirit is the One who manifests God the Father's power in our lives? Maybe we need to look in the mirror and remind ourselves at the beginning of each day that God Almighty—the One who holds all things together—is the One who indwells us by His Spirit (Colossians 1:17). He is the power of God inside us. Do we grasp the magnitude of this for our daily lives?

He Helps Me Do Hard Things

The Holy Spirit is not a lesser version of God. He *is* God. We can do hard things—and endure hard things—not because of anything we bring to the table but because God's Spirit *in us* is more than sufficient for our struggles. *Impossible* is not in His vocabulary. The Holy Spirit reminds us what has been "freely given to us," which is God's power that enables us to face whatever the enemy throws our way.

I need to know that the Holy Spirit is more than a traveling companion on the journey of life. I need to know He's both the compass and the map for the journey. Not only that, I need to know that He's the fuel.

I need to know this when I'm at the end of my rope after a hard day with the kids, and I take a deep breath, close my eyes, and remember that God is in me.

I need to know, in times of crisis, when a family member is facing illness or I can't fix the pain of a child who has been hurt by his friends, that the Holy Spirit is coursing through them. Knowing this makes a difference!

For example, I was recently having a conversation with one of my dearest friends about the characteristics of the Holy Spirit, and she shared a powerful story with me that I want to pass along.

She told me about the way her mother would always remind her that the power of the Holy Spirit was in her when she was facing challenges or struggles. Her mom would say things like, "You have the Holy Spirit! Remember that. God's power is inside you, so you don't have anything to fear!"

My friend didn't comprehend the magnitude of that encouragement when she was young, but that seed was planted in her; this friend of mine is one of the most fearless women I know, and she can now trace her fearlessness to her mother's encouragement in her younger days that God's power was in her and for her benefit.

The same goes for you and me. He isn't just hanging out beside us, like our best girlfriend, but He is in the midst of our very being. As you wash the fifteenth load of laundry, strive to meet deadlines, await news from the doctor, battle a chronic illness, have the hard conversations, find the courage within you to ask for forgiveness, water the plants, and watch the sunrise, He is there. He is more than your companion; He is God and your source of supernatural power.

He Enables Me to Love God

Another unique function of God the Spirit is how He enables us to love God the Father. Without Him, we cannot love God the Father. This is good reason to pause and thank Him! "Thank you, Holy Spirit, for this priceless enablement. Without you, I would not know the love that changes everything."

Jesus laid down His sinless life and paid the ultimate price for us to receive God's unwavering love—a love that has no asterisk pointing us to fine print at the bottom of the page that defines the exceptions to this love. That purchase was the work of Christ alone. He rescued us and redeemed us.

The Holy Spirit applies the love that Christ secured. He puts it into full operation in our lives. He makes it real to us. He makes it alive in us.

Do you want to encounter God the Father in a more intimate way? This is what God the Spirit does. Can we just sit with that for a second? We can have a warm, closely personal relationship with the King. God the Holy Spirit is the One who makes this possible, and it's His pleasure to do so. He lets us in on their love.

What a privilege! And I just can't help but wonder how our openness to the Spirit would change if we saw His presence as a privilege in our lives. But now we're starting to talk about His personhood, so let's turn the page to discover the Person of the Holy Spirit, and the priceless treasure we've been given in His friendship.

Last but Not Least

Reflect: Remember how my friend said her mom would give her pep talks when she was little? She'd say, "Honey, you have the Holy Spirit! You remember that! God's power is inside you. You don't have anything to fear!" Where in your life do you need to know that's true today?

Respond: Today, borrow that pep talk and give it to yourself or pass it along to a friend who needs to know that the Holy Spirit is present and powerful, accessible and *alive!*

five

He Is a Person

I was recently in Nashville, a town I absolutely love visiting, for a few work-related events, and I made sure to add an extra night to my trip to visit with friends and relax. I have a few favorite spots I frequent when I visit, one being an adorable boutique in Green Hills called K McCarthy.

While aimlessly roaming the boutique, I stumbled upon a beautiful painting of a dove. It was so lovely that I motioned to my friend Courtney, whom I was shopping with, to come admire the artwork with me. Courtney knew I was preoccupied with the Spirit, so she wasn't surprised when I said, "You have to come over here to see this beautiful painting of the Holy Spirit." If I hadn't been getting on a plane later that day with nowhere to put the painting, I likely would have made an impulsive purchase!

But even as the words "painting of the Holy Spirit" fell from my lips, I was reminded how easy it is to reduce the Holy Spirit to a symbol rather than to explore the actual *person* of the Spirit.

Symbols for the Holy Spirit

There are several symbols used to depict the Holy Spirit.

In most cases, the Holy Spirit is symbolized —or portrayed—as a dove because He descended upon Jesus like a dove when Jesus emerged from the Jordan after being baptized by John (Mark 1:10).

The Holy Spirit is also often depicted as wind and fire because later, in the book of Acts, while the disciples were praying and waiting for the Holy Spirit to come, we read "there came from heaven a sound like a mighty rushing wind, and it filled the entire house where they were sitting. And divided tongues as of fire appeared to them and rested on each one of them" (2:2–3).

In John 3:8 we see imagery of the Holy Spirit as wind again. John writes, "The wind blows where it wishes, and you hear its sound, but you do not know where it comes from or where it goes. So it is with everyone who is born of the Spirit." The Greek word for wind, *pneuma*, is also used for Spirit. And how the wind blows is much like how the Spirit works. You can't control Him, but you can see His effects and you can feel His power. Indeed, He is as mysterious as He is made-known.

> You can't control Him, but you can see His effects and you can feel His power.

One final depiction of the Spirit worth mentioning is water. This is because Jesus himself likened the Holy Spirit to a well of living water when He said, "If anyone thirsts, let him come to me and drink. Whoever believes in me, as the Scripture has said, 'Out of his heart will flow rivers of living water'" (John 7:37–38). We know He was speaking of the Spirit here because of v. 39: "Now this he said about the Spirit, whom those who believed in him were to receive, for as yet the Spirit had not been given, because Jesus was not yet glorified." We will dig deeper into this story later, but it's good for us to know now that "rivers of living water" was said in relation to the Spirit.

We are born thirsty. Just look around. We are all searching for something to satisfy our parched souls. And Jesus is inviting us to drink from Him—the only true refreshment—because He quenches our thirst with the eternal, bottomless well of His Spirit. We will stay thirsty until we drink from Him and know the refreshment of His Spirit.

So it's easy to see why—and how—the Holy Spirit is often mistaken as the things by which He was symbolized in Scripture. What we need to know is that these symbols are used to show the disposition, character, and work of the Holy Spirit—that these symbols are how He *presented* himself—but He is not confined to any of the symbols. He is a *person*—with a personality—who is wholly distinct from those things. He is a person who has all three components that comprise a personality—a mind, a will, and emotions.

It's probably also worth mentioning why we refer to the Holy Spirit as "He." We use the masculine pronouns when speaking about Him because this is how Scripture reveals Him and how Jesus speaks about Him. As just one of countless examples, we can turn to John 16:7–14 and read eleven instances of the Spirit being referred to with the masculine pronouns *He*, *His*, and *Him*.

He Has a Personality

One of my favorite books, *Beautiful Outlaw* by John Eldredge, invites us in its subtitle to experience "the playful, disruptive, extravagant personality of Jesus." I read it many years ago and it had a profound impact on how I understood the *personhood* of Jesus. Story after story shows how Jesus—God made flesh—has the most incredibly dynamic personality. Throughout the Gospels we see how Jesus walked this earth as fully human, and fully experienced the joys and the sorrows we encounter today.

One of the most hard-to-read verses in the Bible is one that most clearly demonstrates His personhood: When Jesus knew the crucifixion was imminent, He said to His disciples, "My soul is crushed with grief to the point of death. Stay here and keep watch with me" (Matthew 26:38 NLT). Jesus knew grief in His soul like we will never know.

Contrast that heartbreak with one of the most hope-filled verses in the Bible, where Matthew pens these words of God: "Behold, my servant whom I have chosen, my beloved with whom my soul is well pleased. I will put my Spirit upon him, and he will proclaim justice to the Gentiles" (Matthew 12:18). God makes it known that He has a soul, and it is utterly delighted with His Son, Jesus.

So we know God has a soul and we know Jesus has a soul, but I think it's harder for us to imagine the Holy Spirit having evidence of a soul, partly because of the imagery used to depict the Spirit. How do wind and fire and water have a soul? But remember, He isn't any of those things. He's a person with a personality.

> Knowing the Spirit has a personality matters because we can't have a relationship with a symbol.

Knowing the Spirit has a personality matters because we can't have a relationship with a symbol. We can only have a relationship with a person, and that is precisely what we can have with the person of the Holy Spirit—a deeply personal friendship.

His personhood proves He understands us. I find that absolutely incredible. The Holy Spirit *gets* you. He gets me. Don't we all long to be understood? Think about how affirming and comforting it feels when a friend is able to say "I understand" or "I completely get that!" That is what our friend the Holy Spirit says. He not only gets us, but He can be trusted with our hearts!

As your closest friend, He knows you better than any other, and you can be completely at ease with Him. But being at ease with Him is not the same thing as being yielded to Him. Just like you can hurt a friend, you can hurt the Holy Spirit. It remains true that you can never lose Him or be abandoned by Him, but you can grieve Him and diminish the sense of His presence in your life.

"To put it another way: the Holy Spirit is in you if you are a Christian (Romans 8:9). But it does not follow that He is always in you *ungrieved*. The Holy Spirit won't bend the rules for any of us. He is no respecter of persons. He will not adjust to any of us. He favors no human being. We must adjust to *Him*. We must adjust to His ways," writes R. T. Kendall.[1]

Grieving the Holy Spirit

When someone is grieving, it means they are experiencing deep sorrow resulting from loss, but loss does not have to mean death. It can be the loss of a bond where deep affection and connection existed.

This is why Paul wrote, "Do not grieve the Holy Spirit of God, by whom you were sealed for the day of redemption" (Ephesians 4:30). "The Greek word *lupeo* can mean 'get your feelings hurt.'"[2] So Paul is essentially pleading with us not to hurt the Holy Spirit, who is sensitive to our sin.

The Holy Spirit is hurt when He must coexist with our intentional sin—the things we do that are incompatible with His character. And when we hurt Him, the bond of affection and connection with us is interrupted. He is that sensitive to our willful sin. One of the reasons He grieves is because He knows how our sins bring grief to our souls. This is His "for us" love.

> He grieves because He knows how our sins bring grief to our souls.

Years ago, I learned that sin is not just breaking the rules of God, it's breaking the heart of God. That new lens through which to view my behavior made a profound difference in how I dealt with sin in my life. Discovering that I grieve the Holy Spirit—that I deeply wound

Him—with specific behaviors and actions had a similar impact on me.

What behavior grieves Him in such a painful way?

Paul answers this question in the next verse: "Let all bitterness and wrath and anger and clamor and slander be put away from you, along with all malice" (Ephesians 4:31).

What I found so fascinating is that the specific sins that grieve the Holy Spirit all relate to how we treat one another. There is a relational theme in the list Paul lays out, beginning with bitterness. This was no small thing for me to discover. Let me tell you why.

Getting Rid of Bitterness

My husband, Mike, and I believe in marriage counseling. Some call it marriage coaching. But whatever you call it, we believe in it. It has helped us immensely in our seventeen years of marriage. We've gone to counseling when things were good because they can always be better. We want us to be the best us. And we've gone when things were hard because, if we can just be honest here, marriage can be complicated, no matter how crazy about each other you are.

In one of the seasons when things were hard, Mike and I went to see our marriage counselor. We weren't walking through anything that is out of the ordinary for two people who love each other deeply, but we had let the business of life and raising lots of humans get in the way of making us a priority, and I was feeling bitter. This is where counseling has been especially helpful. I love the space our counselor creates for us to have vulnerable conversations and to see our situation through one another's eyes.

I should pause here and tell you that I knew the Holy Spirit was going to get in my business when I started writing this book, and I thought I mostly knew what that would look like. But as I began to study the ways in which we grieve the Spirit of God,

I sensed that bitterness was going to be one of the Spirit's first orders of business with me. And indeed it was, right there in that counseling room.

The Holy Spirit was lovingly convicting me as I listened to Mike speak. I sensed the Spirit saying to me, "When you hold onto bitterness in your marriage—over even the smallest things—you don't just grieve Mike, you grieve Me. You don't just lose emotional intimacy with him, you lose intimacy with Me."

In that moment, I saw Mike as more than my husband. I saw him as someone who also had the living Holy Spirit inside him. And it was only by the power of the Holy Spirit that all the bitterness and self-righteousness I was harboring as I walked into that counseling room dissipated. The Holy Spirit freed me to forgive, and to seek forgiveness.

Not only did I not want to keep living in diminished emotional intimacy with my man, I didn't want to lose the new sense of closeness and connection I was developing with the Spirit. I didn't want to grieve Him.

Welcoming His Work

Welcoming this work of the Spirit requires sensitivity to His presence and a posture of humility with people. If we don't want to see our flaws, and we are even more hesitant to confess them, we impede the Spirit's work in our lives. Maybe the question we have to ask ourselves is, "Is this worth grieving my best friend?" when we walk in intentional sin and, even more so, live in unforgiveness of sins committed against us.

The personhood of the Holy Spirit became very real to me in that session, and it's no exaggeration to say I haven't been the same since. I haven't mastered releasing bitterness and offering forgiveness, but I'm not who I was.

When we force the Holy Spirit to coexist with bitterness and other behaviors that relate to how we treat one another—such as rage, anger, harsh words, and slander—we cause Him sorrow, and the intimacy diminishes.

So then how are we to strengthen and nourish our friendship with the Spirit? "Be kind to one another, tenderhearted, forgiving one another, as God in Christ forgave you" (Ephesians 4:32). All of which can be accomplished through His supernatural empowerment.

last but not least

Reflect: Read Romans 8:26–27. What do these verses suggest about the Holy Spirit's personhood and His affection toward you?

Respond: Think about the ways you've viewed the Holy Spirit in the past—perhaps as wind, fire, or a dove. Close your eyes and let Him develop in His true form—as a person with a soul, and with a heart that beats for you.

six

He Is Equal

A few years back I was invited to speak at a church conference with a theme I was excited to study and teach on. But before I accepted the invitation, I jumped on a quick call with the conference coordinator to get a better feel for how they wanted me to script the sessions.

She explained that they wanted the conference to be a place where all women, no matter where they were—or weren't—in their walk of faith, would feel comfortable. I got that. She then explained that in my teaching it would be good to talk about God ("Of course," I said), and it would be okay to speak about Jesus (yes, absolutely agreed), but they needed me to steer clear of speaking about the Holy Spirit (uh-oh). "Speaking about the Spirit could make some people really uncomfortable, so we'd rather you stick to God and Jesus," was the message she relayed.

While I understood her concern, I gently tried to explain that I believe the solution isn't to avoid speaking about the Spirit of God, but rather to seek to remove the fear and distrust we have about Him, and to reveal the significance of His work in wooing our hearts to Jesus and His power to transform our lives in a beautiful way. I can't teach the Gospel and not mention the grandeur of the Spirit of God. Women are trying to transform their lives in their own strength, but what we really need is the Spirit's power to produce supernatural results.

Thankfully, she chose to trust me, and we got to witness God do a mighty work in our midst.

But the sentiments held by that confer- ence coordinator are not uncommon. We are afraid of the supernatural work of the Spirit because of commonly held stereotypes.

> The Father, Son, and Holy Spirit are as equal as they are eternal.

Or because of witnessed abuse of His power. But I think it's more than that. Beyond His name being used and abused, we aren't sure He is of equal value in our lives. The Holy Spirit is so often treated as inferior. He is treated as the least valu- able in the Trinity, when actually, He is utterly invaluable in the Christian life.

One commonly held theory about His inferiority is that because His work is the last to be emphasized in Scripture, He is the least significant in the Trinity. But a thorough study of Scripture reveals the Father, Son, and Holy Spirit are as equal as they are eternal.

He Is Equal *and* Eternal

Let me share a silly example but one that I think will resonate. Consider how parents typically introduce their children. Do they name them in order of significance? (Could you even imagine?) "These are our children. This is Tommy. He was born first and I'm introducing him first because he is the most special and im- portant child in our family. Next is little Teddy. He is second in significance in our family, but he was actually born last. And then this is our middle daughter, Minnie. I introduce her last because, well, she is the least valuable in our family." The order in which parents list their children doesn't represent their significance in the family. (Or at least we hope not!) Likewise, the progressive revelation of God the Father, God the Son, and God the Holy Spirit does not represent their significance in the Godhead, as is sometimes suggested. We see the significance of the Spirit's work throughout all of Scripture, starting in Genesis 1:1! But it *is* fair to say that the Spirit's work is most emphasized and visible from the Day of Pentecost (in Acts) forward, when the Holy Spirit did more than rest upon people—He took up residence inside them.

Both the Old and New Testaments attest to the Holy Spirit being an equal member of the Trinity. One prime example from the Old Testament is found in Deuteronomy 6:4, which is the central verse of Israel's faith (called the Shema). We read, "Hear, O Israel: The LORD our God, the LORD is One." Meaning, one God in three divine and equal persons.

In the New Testament, we see them equally working together in many of the passages we will explore shortly, but the most interesting to me is the Great Commission, the last recorded instruction given by Jesus to His disciples before His ascension. This is one of the most significant places where we see the equality of the Three-In-One.

Matthew writes, "Then Jesus came to them and said, "All authority in heaven and on earth has been given to me. Therefore go and make disciples of all nations, baptizing them in the name of the Father and of the Son and of the Holy Spirit, and teaching them to obey everything I have commanded you. And surely I am with you always, to the very end of the age" (28:18–20 NIV).

Jesus taught His disciples to baptize in the threefold name of Father, Son, *and* Holy Spirit.

He Is Equal *and* Essential

Why does it matter that we understand Him to be equal? Because He is absolutely essential to the dynamic and thriving life of the Christian. We cannot flourish without the Spirit. Our lack of attention to and affection for all that He is designed to do in our lives leaves us powerless to live "life to the fullest," as Jesus came to give us. Our faith will flourish to the extent that we are filled with the Spirit.

What are some signs that we've neglected or forgotten the essentiality of the Spirit? When our faith feels dry or stagnant. When we find ourselves stuck in behaviors and patterns from which we've been set free. When toxic thoughts take up residence in our minds. When we put ourselves on the throne, seeking praise and glory that isn't ours.

> We cannot flourish without the Spirit.

But beyond that, to neglect Him and treat Him as the inferior part of God is insulting to the Trinity and inconsistent with Scripture. Understanding the essentiality and beauty of the Spirit will profoundly enhance our lives and our walks with Jesus. We need Him!

In the words of Augustine of Hippo, "As they are inseparable, so they work inseparably."[1]

But Isn't Jesus Enough?

One of the questions Francis Chan poses in *Forgotten God* is, "I've got Jesus. Why do I need the Spirit?"[2] That question struck a chord with me, and I wrestled with it before I read how he answered it. But the truth is, I didn't have good answers. Or at least not answers that satisfied me.

What we need to understand is that if we are trying to be a witness for Christ and grow in the likeness of Christ without the power of Christ—the Holy Spirit—we will remain frustrated and discouraged. We only get so far without the Spirit's help. No matter how hard we strive, human effort cannot produce supernatural results.

We can determine to be more patient, but without the Spirit, our ability to remain calm when dealing with a difficult situation or person will run dry. We can determine to be more loving, but our capacity to love the unlovable will not reflect the kind of love Jesus modeled. We can determine to be more disciplined, but our power over temptation will only take us so far. We don't need more willpower. We need more Spirit-power.

This is why it's not enough to acknowledge His existence but avoid Him as part of the Christian experience. We rob ourselves from experiencing the power of God when we neglect the significance of the Holy Spirit's work.

> We don't need more willpower. We need more Spirit-power.

So why do we need the Spirit if we have Jesus? Because, as Billy Graham wrote, "We need the work of the Son of God *for* us, and the work of the Spirit of God *in* us."[3] This is the undeniable truth witnessed on the Day of Pentecost and throughout the book of Acts.

What Difference Did Pentecost Make?

Pentecost was the birth of the church and the beginning of the work of the Spirit in the present age. The function and work of the Spirit pre-Pentecost differed from His work post-Pentecost.

As we will see, the power of the Spirit at Pentecost was in *far* greater measure than anything they'd experienced previously.

The Day of Pentecost is when the Holy Spirit descended in the Upper Room in Jerusalem. One hundred and twenty of Christ's core followers, including His disciples, were eagerly awaiting Him, just as Jesus had told them to do. And when the Holy Spirit descended, He filled them with His supernatural power, just as Jesus said He would.

Pentecost occurred fifty days after Jesus' resurrection and ten days after His ascension. This was the day that changed everything, and I don't say that lightly. Lives were instantly and dramatically transformed. Peter is the perfect case study for why we need the Spirit when we already have Jesus. Peter, who had recently been terrified to even be associated with Jesus, was utterly transformed when the Holy Spirit was poured into him. The opinions of others no longer mattered to him and he preached the Gospel with conviction and clarity.

We will look more closely at Pentecost and Peter's story soon, but for now I want to consider another important aspect of the Spirit's equality. Because not only is He equal with the Father and Son, but He is equally available and accessible to every person who has put their trust in Jesus and received salvation.

He Is Equally Available

His power is just as available to the Christian who is leading Bible studies as it is to the Christian who is just learning how to read the Bible. He is equally available to the Christian who's been following Jesus since they were a child as He is to the Christian who just put their trust in Jesus. There are no prequalifiers to His availability other than putting your trust in Jesus. If you have put your trust in the Son of God, the Spirit of God is fully available to you, and He wants to show you the supernatural work He can do in you and through you! The question is, will you let Him?

Because here's the thing: Equally available doesn't mean equally active. We play an important role in His activity in our life!

> Equally available doesn't mean equally active.

Robert Morris puts it well: "Having the Holy Spirit's power available to us isn't the same thing as making ourselves available to the Holy Spirit's life-changing power. We have to yield. Our stubborn, prideful selves have to submit. We have to receive."[4]

Indeed, the Holy Spirit is the last to be named—but not the least in significance—in the Trinity. Last but not least! This is the perspective shift we all need if we want to receive the blessings available to every believer.

last but not least

Reflect: Read John 14:16, John 14:26, and John 15:26. Notice how all three members of the Trinity are present in each verse. What does this suggest to you about the essential nature of the Spirit in the life of a flourishing Christian?

Respond: Try this when you pray today. Direct your prayers to all three members of the Trinity, speaking directly with God the Father, God the Son, and—*last but not least*—God the Holy Spirit.

seven

He Is Better Than Self-Help

I closed the door behind me, ensured it locked so my hotel room was secure, and I headed toward the elevator. I had a full-day conference ahead of me and I was excited to meet new friends, connect with old ones, and share the message God had placed on my heart.

Stepping off the elevator into the bustling lobby, I went straight to the coffee bar and made a large coffee—so large, in fact, that the friend I ran into while pouring my coffee laughed about the size of my cup compared with the frame of my body. I'm small in stature but my cup was not, because this girl needs her caffeine. Realizing I still had a few minutes to spare, I checked my phone before walking to my car. And that's when it happened. I got the "low-power mode" notification. This didn't make any sense, since I charged my phone while I slept, but something must have gone wrong because the short yellow bar in the top right corner of my phone affirmed what I feared. My phone was close to shutting down and, until then, I'd be running on low power.

Most of us will do just about anything to avoid having to use our phone in low-power mode. We'll borrow a charger from a stranger or purchase a portable power stick at the store. Who wants low productivity with frustrating results? And yet, this is how many of us have become used to living the Christian life. In the yellow zone. Low power. Little productivity. Limited capability. Frustrating results.

I don't think it's a stretch to compare the low-power mode on our phones with the self-help approach to life.

In fact, it seems that one of the most creative tools of the enemy has been convincing us we don't need the power of the very person Jesus said would give us "everything we need for a godly life" (2 Peter 1:3 NIV). We've been tricked into operating in low-power mode, settling for helping ourselves rather than receiving the Spirit's far superior help.

Fighting Our Battles

In our desire to have more strength in our struggles and more control over our circumstances, we might listen to voices who swear the answer is found in striving to be the superheroes of our stories. We are encouraged to give ourselves pep talks about our own greatness, all for our own glory. All the while, *Almighty* God indwells us and is eager to empower us to fight our battles in His might for His name. From the beginning of time we were designed by our Creator to live powered by His Spirit.

> He has given us the Holy Spirit to help us *along*, so let's stop settling for doing it *alone*. We need Holy-help.

He has given us the Holy Spirit to help us *along*, so let's stop settling for doing it *alone*. We need Holy-help.

My intention isn't to undermine the myriad of ways we can be bettered by taking intentional steps to grow, but the Spirit helps us like no superhero cape tied around our neck ever could. I mean, yes, it's fun and helpful to flex our muscles, repeat a few affirming mantras, and drink out of mugs that tells us we're boss babes, but that only gets us so far. Yes, it gets us somewhere we weren't before, but only the really honest will admit it's not as far as we'd like to go. It's not freedom from relying on the flesh to do what only the Spirit can accomplish.

Not only does the Holy Spirit free us from the unbearable burden of fixing ourselves, He frees us from trying to fix those around us, including our spouses, our kids, our parents, our friends, and our leaders. That's His job, and He's really good at it.

Of course, this isn't an excuse to stop being intentional in taking steps to become more of who we were made to be. We know we cannot do nothing and expect something. This isn't a challenge to call on the Holy Spirit, then kick up our feet and turn on Netflix and expect radical life change.

Rather, it's an invitation to be freed from putting all our hope in ourselves. We've been freed from the pressure to be our own savior. We have a greater help, a supernatural help, the One Jesus himself called "the Helper."

Because Self Falls Short of Spirit

Jennie Allen speaks poignantly to this in her phenomenal book *Get Out of Your Head*, when she writes,

> The world understands that no progress can be made without doing the work. They understand it better than many Christians do. But self-help can offer only a better version of yourself; Christ is after a whole new you. God in you. The mind of Christ.
>
> But we don't do it merely as another self-improvement project. We do it because we want to live a new-creation kind of life, a life that truly matters, a life in Christ that God has promised.[1]

This full and meaningful and free life that God has promised and Jennie points to is completely possible, but only through the power of the Holy Spirit.

The best self-help strategy is admitting how much the self needs the Spirit for authentic, lasting, radical change. Self-reliance, self-confidence, self-sufficiency, self-anything falls short of what the Spirit can do. This is why Jesus said, "What gives life is God's Spirit; human power is of no use at all" (John 6:63 GNT).

For example, maybe you've heard the expression "God helps those who help themselves." The reason you won't find a Bible verse attached to that quote is because it's inconsistent with the Gospel message. Here's the Gospel: God helps those who know how much help they need! All we bring is our need. All God needs to show off His power is someone who has come to the end of themselves and knows how powerless they are to produce change without Him.

His Unstoppable Strength

Have you ever considered that the Spirit wants to do far more for you than even you want to do for you? It's true. What He can do is far better, and the outcomes are far bigger, than what we can do on our own!

We see this illustrated when the Lord says to Zerubbabel, "Not by might, nor by power, but by my Spirit, says the LORD of hosts" (Zechariah 4:6).

In this passage, God is promising Zerubbabel that He will see to it that the temple *He* started would be completed and His blessing would be restored, and this would all be accomplished through the matchless power of *His* Spirit, not reliant on Zerubbabel's human power or capacity. The power of His Spirit would finish what He started. The principle being taught here holds true for us now.

Just as the Holy Spirit would enable and empower Zerubbabel to rebuild the temple, so the Holy Spirit will enable and empower us to fulfill what God has planned and prepared for us. He finishes what He starts. That is really good news for us today.

I wonder what things are in front of you, even now, as you hold this book in your hands, that feel too big for you. What feels overwhelming and impossible? Maybe it's what is required of you as a parent. Maybe it's a dying marriage that feels unrevivable. Maybe it's an addiction or a thought pattern that needs healing and breakthrough. Maybe it's a dream God put on your heart—to start a new business or ministry, serve your church, step out of your comfort zone and mentor younger women, or even step back!

As I shared earlier, this book felt far beyond anything I was capable of accomplishing, and honestly, it was. As I near the end of writing it and sneak this paragraph in during final edits, I can assuredly tell you this was far bigger than I realized. But so is my God. So is His power. And if we don't engage His help, we will never know the greatness of that power.

Who's Doing the Work?

I recently ran into a friend I hadn't seen in a few weeks. I know she's been going through a tumultuous time, so after some brief small talk I said, "Friend, can I ask, how's your heart?"

That's when her guard came down and she shared all the ways it feels like her life is crumbling around her. But then she concluded with a positivity I could tell she didn't believe when she said, "But I'm working on myself!"

As I listened to her share what's been going on, I sensed the Holy Spirit nudging me to tell her what He's been teaching me about needing His help, but out of fear of sounding judgmental, I settled for saying something like, "There is so much I admire about you. I know this has been so hard on you. I think it's incredible that you've found the strength to work *on* yourself!"

"Jeannie," she prodded with a smile, "I know you too well. I can tell there is something else you want to say. Please say it." "Okay," I said, hesitantly. "What if the Holy Spirit wants to work *in* you while you work *on* you? What if you let Him do that? You don't have to do the hard work of healing without His help."

I assured my friend I understand the struggle to rely on the Spirit, because I am prone to settling for only what I can do. I work on being a more patient mom, I work on being a more loving and supportive wife, I work on being more self-controlled with the things I enjoy, I work on being more grateful for what I've been given, I work on being more joyful in trying circumstances . . . and the list goes on. But I do it without inviting the Holy Spirit to work *in* me.

> "What if the Holy Spirit wants to work *in* you while you work *on* you?"

But as intentional as we may be to create internal change in our lives, we can't do it without the transforming power of God.

As human beings, we have limitations. We may not like it and we may fight it, but no matter how hard we try and no matter the lengths to which we're willing to go, we are limited in what we can accomplish and make happen. Our humanity gets in the way.

This is why Paul prays that we would "understand the incredible greatness of God's power for us who believe him. This is the same mighty power that raised Christ from the dead and seated him in the place of honor at God's right hand in the heavenly realms" (Ephesians 1:19–20 NLT).

God is not bound by human limitations. He is all-powerful and unstoppable. And His plan has always been for His children to live in the supernatural power of *His* unlimited, indwelling Spirit.

last but not least

Reflect: What self-help strategies have you been relying on? Can you relate to how the low-power mode on your phone can feel like the self-help approach to life?

Respond: As Paul prayed in the passage we just read, ask God to help you rely on the incredible greatness of His power *in* you. Invite the Holy Spirit to manifest His power *in* you as you work *on* you. Even dare to ask the Holy Spirit to surprise you with the significant difference His supernatural help makes in your life!

eight

He Is Our Guarantee

Are you familiar with *The Five Love Languages*? This book provides helpful categories and names for the ways in which we tend to express and receive love. These five love languages, as described by author Gary Chapman, are words of affirmation, gifts, acts of service, quality time, and physical touch.

One of the most helpful things I learned when I read this book more than twenty years ago is if we want our spouses to feel the love we are seeking to express, we need to know their unique love language, which is rarely the same as ours. Because most of us tend to express love in the same way we prefer to receive it, our expressions of love often are not received by our spouse the way we'd hoped.

One result of reading Chapman's classic was that I suddenly understood why my dad has continued to buy my mom gifts to show his love for her even though she has begged for fifty-nine years and counting, "George, please don't buy me any expensive gifts for special occasions. I don't need anything material." He can't help himself. Lucky for him, his gift-giving has become endearing. The sheer hilarity of some of the gifts he's chosen for my mom (like the porcelain turtle he bought her at the gift shop while on a beach vacation) has brought much laughter to family gatherings. We all took a picture with the turtle before she drove him back to the store to return it! Thankfully, Dad has also learned her unique love language and now speaks it fluently.

Through reading *The Five Love Languages*, I discovered my primary love language is acts of service. Mike knows that if he wants me to feel loved, he shouldn't buy me presents. He should just fold a pile (or two) of laundry or surprise me with a full tank of gas in my car. That's when my heart tank, as well as my gas tank, is full!

But a close second love language for me is words of affirmation. My father wrote me the most beautiful letters of affirmation as I was growing up, and I have them saved in a special box to this day. And now, my boys know that the love notes they write me are the most cherished gifts they give me. Everything else pales in comparison.

One of my favorite ways my husband expresses words of affirmation is when he wraps his arms around my waist and whispers in my ear one single word: "Mine." If you know the just-right combination of tough-and-tender planted in my man, you know "mine" is said gently. It's not one ounce possessive or controlling. It's said with a sense of gratitude and pride that God gave him me. "Mine," he says, with the look of unconditional love in his eyes. Every time he says it, he makes me feel chosen by him all over again. Sometimes he'll see me looking very ordinary, doing very ordinary things, and he'll smile and say, "Mine." In doing so, he reminds me he loves me for me, as messy as I can be.

It was only recently when Mike whispered "Mine" on a day I wasn't feeling the least bit loveable that I remembered this is precisely the same thing that God says about me—with absolute sheer delight—when He looks upon me. The words, "He calls you His own," bounced around in my brain and led me to open my Bible and search for the whole passage, which led me to Ephesians 1, where Paul writes about our spiritual blessings in Christ.

Do we know the spiritual blessings that are part of our inheritance in Christ? "When you believed, you were marked in him with a seal, the promised Holy Spirit, who is a deposit guaranteeing our inheritance until the redemption of those who are God's possession—to the praise of his glory" (Ephesians 1:13–14 NIV).

Paul lays it out like this:

1. You heard the good news that God saves you.
2. When you believed, He fulfilled His promise of giving you the Holy Spirit.
3. The Spirit is how God identifies you as His own.
4. The Spirit inside you is your guarantee.
5. All of this happens so that God gets the glory.

When we believe in Christ, God calls us His own. "Mine." We are marked in Christ with a seal, the promised Holy Spirit. We are God's cherished and chosen possession. I still get undone by this truth. I am God's daughter, a daughter of the King, covered in the righteousness and perfection of Jesus Christ, sealed by the Holy Spirit as a sign that He will finish what He started in me.

Why does this matter? When I lay my head on my pillow, rehearsing all the ways I let my God down again that day, I am assured that the Holy Spirit is the guarantee that God won't give up on me, as sinful as I can be. This unfathomable grace is meant to bring glory to God, the ultimate giver of grace.

The Seal of the Spirit

At the time Paul was writing this, a seal signified security. So let's talk more about this seal.

A seal is an identifying mark intended to authenticate something, such as a document, and it provides assurance of security. When a letter of importance, such as an invitation to a special event, arrives in your mailbox, the envelope may be secured with a wax seal. You've probably also seen a herd of cattle bearing a seal in the form of a brand, which clearly communicates ownership.

But the seal of the Holy Spirit is not a thing, like wax on a document or a hot iron brand on cattle. This seal is a person—the Holy Spirit, attesting that God lovingly says "mine" when He looks upon you and me. The Holy Spirit is the believer's seal, communicating we are securely united to God in Christ.

Why does this seal hold such significance?

I remember being told as a young child by a family friend that if I died with unconfessed sin in my life, my salvation was at stake. Do you know what I did from that moment on? I lived in utter fear, confessing my sin on the daily, or sometimes, on the minute. This was one seriously time-consuming task!

After about a week of this lie being planted in my mind, the fear became too burdensome, and I asked my parents about what I was told. They assured me that what was shared with me was unbiblical, and they pointed me to verses about the Holy Spirit as our guarantee to assure me that my ongoing struggle with sin would never steal my salvation. Relieved doesn't begin to describe the feeling that washed over me.

Blaspheming the Holy Spirit

This is probably a good time to talk about what I've always felt was one of the most frightening verses in the Bible—a verse that can inject fear into the most faithful follower of Jesus. It's the one that talks about the unforgivable sin of blasphemy against the Holy Spirit.

Jesus said, "Therefore I tell you, every sin and blasphemy will be forgiven people, but the blasphemy against the Spirit will not be forgiven" (Matthew 12:31).

> Fear that God will stop calling us His possession if we don't have perfect performance is put to rest in the Holy Spirit's presence.

Unforgivable sin? That sounds terrifying and utterly contradictory to everything else Scripture says about God's grace. So if this verse has put fear in your bones like it has in so many, let's put our fear to rest now.

"Blasphemy against the Holy Spirit is the unchanging conviction that Jesus is evil. In essence, the only unforgivable sin is a conclusive rejection of Christ rather than a contrite reception of Him."[1] "One blasphemes the Holy Spirit by finally denying that Jesus is God in the flesh—or saying that Jesus has an evil spirit. How can you know that you have not committed this unpardonable sin? If you can testify from your heart that Jesus is God, worry no more!"[2]

This is what we need to know: The seal of the Holy Spirit identifies us as God's possession and guarantees our eternal security in Christ. If we bear this seal, we never—ever—have to fear committing the unforgivable sin of blasphemy.

Our Guarantee

The Holy Spirit bearing witness with our spirit that we belong to God brings confidence to the Christian. Fear that God will stop calling us His possession if we don't have perfect performance is put to rest in the Holy Spirit's presence. He has "put his seal on us and given us his Spirit in our hearts as a guarantee" (2 Corinthians 1:22). A guarantee! You can be absolutely confident that on the days when you seek Him with all your heart, as well as on the days when you wander off like a lost sheep, He promises you will receive everything He *has* for you because of what Jesus *did* for you.

last but not least

Reflect: Have you ever felt fear that your past mistakes or the sins you commit on a daily basis will keep you from eternal life in heaven? Read 2 Corinthians 1:20–22. What reassurance does this provide you?

Respond: You, my friend, are signed, sealed, and delivered. Take a ballpoint pen and gently draw a simple cross on the inside of your wrist, or sketch a cross on a sticky note and post it on your mirror, as a reminder that you belong to Jesus . . . forever.

nine

He Makes Much of Jesus

I'm going to be bold with you as we walk through these pages. I hope that's okay. And sometimes that's going to mean calling out things we'd rather not remember, like the fact that we have a very real enemy who does not want us discovering the irresistibility of Christ.

The enemy's highest priority is to keep us from receiving salvation through Christ. There is nothing the "prowling lion" wants more than to keep you and me from inheriting the eternal blessings we receive in Christ. But, oh, once he loses that battle, he does not quit. He doubles down.

Once we are new creations in Christ, I believe the enemy's highest priority becomes ensuring we don't experience the *freedom* and *fullness* of God, meaning he'll work to make sure we keep not just one but both hands up against God's Spirit, saying, "I don't really *get* you, so I don't really *need* you."

In stark contrast to the enemy's goal is the Spirit's. The Holy Spirit makes much of Jesus. The Holy Spirit is the One who woos us to Christ, magnifies the beauty of Christ, and produces Christlikeness in our lives. His goal is to glorify Jesus.

Jesus said, "He will glorify me because it is from me that he will receive what he will make known to you. All that belongs to the Father is mine. That is why I said the Spirit will receive from me what he will make known to you" (John 16:14–15 NIV).

> His goal is to glorify Jesus.

"The Holy Spirit's task, then, is to unfold the meaning of Jesus's person and work to believers in such a way that the glory of it—its infinite importance and beauty—is brought home to the mind and heart."[1]

So of course the enemy is going to work relentlessly to ensure we neglect the Holy Spirit! The Spirit's ministry is so very dangerous to the enemy's mission to not only draw us away from Christ, but also to destroy us in the process.

The Enemy's Goal

And just to be clear, what I've had to confront in my own life is that the enemy's work usually isn't all that obvious. Maybe we aren't running toward destruction and sending warning signals to those who love us that we're caught in his snare. But if we're being completely honest, we know what other loves we have placed above Jesus. Maybe it's the love of money or comfort. Maybe it's success, or status, or substances. Maybe it's our spouse or our children. We strive to fill our unsatisfied souls with people and pleasures and possessions, when our souls are crying out for more of Jesus. Indeed, the enemy has sold us a bill of goods about what will satisfy us.

Or perhaps the enemy's work looks more like convincing us the Spirit is superfluous. He knows he can't draw us away from Jesus, but he'll see to it that we settle for a faith that lacks the Spirit's power. In doing so, we settle for discontentment and dissatisfaction. We settle for rote religion and stale sentiments. We know all the things we're supposed to say and believe about Jesus, but they're not making a meaningful difference in our lives. Not only is such an existence far short of the dynamic life we were made to experience in Christ, but this lifeless faith doesn't draw others to the Gospel because they don't see anything in us that they don't already possess.

Friend, we cannot, we will not, let the enemy have his way in making the Holy Spirit seem pointless or inaccessible to us. This is war, and there is too much at stake. Through God's indwelling Spirit, we are empowered with His glorious unlimited resources. We can't miss this! Everything we need to live like Christ is given to us through the indwelling Spirit of God. So *of course* the enemy works to ensure we ignore or reject the Spirit in our life.

Paul's Prayer for Us to Know God's Love

Years ago, while I was writing my first book and discovering all I'd been missing about how wild and unfathomable God's grace is, I began a routine of praying Ephesians 3:16–20 over my kids. As a mom who previously spent a lot of time teaching my little kids how to obey the *law* of God, I was now desperate to ensure they knew the inexhaustible *love* of God above all else. As I began to experience its transforming and freeing power in my own life, I knew the love of Jesus had to be the foundation on which my children's faith was built.

I eventually asked an artist to paint the verses (in the NLV) on a white wooden sign that now hangs in our kitchen, and I still pray this prayer—that Paul prayed for the Ephesians—over each of my kids in the morning:

> I pray that because of the riches of His shining-greatness, He will make you strong with power in your hearts through the Holy Spirit.
> I pray that Christ may live in your hearts by faith. I pray that you will be filled with love.

I pray that you will be able to understand how wide and how
long and how high and how deep His love is.
I pray that you will know the love of Christ. His love goes beyond anything we can understand. I pray that you will be filled
with God Himself.
God is able to do much more than we ask or think through His
power working in us.

When I chose this passage for our family, I knew that Paul's
prayer was about us knowing the wild love of Jesus. What I missed,
however, was *how* Paul said we'd come to know this love. I still
thought it was mostly on me to open my children's hearts to His
love!

But let's see how these verses actually play out:

What does Paul pray for? He prays that we would be
strengthened with power in our inner being.
How does Paul say this will happen? Through the Holy
Spirit.
Why does Paul want us to experience this Spirit-given
strengthening in our inner being? So that we will have the
ability to grasp the ungraspable love of Jesus!

This is nothing short of glorious! The Spirit of God awakens us
to the inexhaustible love of Jesus that "goes beyond anything we
can understand." And the result of us receiving this love is we *get
to* experience God doing beyond what we could ask or imagine,
all for the glory of His name.

This is the good stuff the enemy is determined to make us miss
out on. The questions we have to answer are these: Will I let him
win, or am I all in? Do I want to open myself up to the One Jesus
said is "to my advantage" and "for my good," or keep Him at
arm's length?

The Holy Spirit's Priority

The more I've come to know the incomprehensible friend I have in the Spirit, and how He's been there all along, the deeper my gratitude grows for what Jesus did for me. And now it makes so much sense to me how the Holy Spirit exists to make much of Jesus. He doesn't want the spotlight or the glory. He shines it on Jesus, the One who laid down His life to rescue us.

R. T. Kendall explains,

> It is not the Spirit who is to be focused on when it comes to glory. You may ask: "Is not the Holy Spirit God?" Yes. But it was not the Holy Spirit who died. It is not the Holy Spirit to whom every knee shall bow one day. So when Jesus said that the Holy Spirit would take what is "mine," He was stating that the focus would be on the Redeemer and Savior of the world who would be glorified and made known to us.[2]

Why does this matter? Because just as the Holy Spirit's goal is to put the spotlight on Jesus, it's the Holy Spirit *in us* that makes us want to take the spotlight off ourselves and put it on Jesus.

I don't know about you, but I can be good at being a glory hoarder. You know when I've seen the worst in me? When I don't get the credit for things I've said or done. Glory hoarding is the stuff the Spirit has to snuff out in us, and He does it by becoming larger inside of us.

The Holy Spirit changes our desires from wanting to be worshiped to wanting to worship the only One worthy of praise. A self-glorifying life is a certain sign that we lack the activity of the Holy Spirit. And a God-glorifying life is a certain sign of the Spirit's activity.

Putting the Spotlight on Jesus

Jesus taught His disciples this principle in John 15:26–27 (NIV):

But I will send you the Advocate—the Spirit of truth. He will come to you from the Father and will testify all about me. And you must also testify about me because you have been with me from the beginning of my ministry.

Jesus affirms that the ultimate aim of the Holy Spirit is to point people to Him. To testify to who He is and what He accomplished. And then He affirms how the disciples—and now we—partner with Him in that work when He says, "And you must also testify about me."

Do you want your life to be a love song for Jesus? Do you want your life to point people to the goodness of your God? Good grief, I do! I want it more than anything else. And I bet you do too. So let's ask the Holy Spirit together to make His aim our aim! And then let's thank Him again for this glorious reality:

The *assurance* we have *in* Jesus and the *affection* we feel *for* Jesus is produced by the Holy Spirit.

last but not least

Reflect: Read John 15:26–27. What does Jesus say the Holy Spirit will do? And what does Jesus say we must also do?

Respond: Jesus calls us to testify. Sometime this week, make it a point to step out of your comfort zone by shining the spotlight on Jesus for someone who needs to know His love.

ten

He Authored the Bible

When someone recommends a book to me, especially a nonfiction book, one of the first questions I usually ask is, "Who's the author?" The author of the book is just as important to me, if not more so, than the topic of the book, because I want to know the author is someone I can trust to give me solid truth. If I don't know the author, I will look at who endorsed the book.

There is only one author, however, whom we know we can trust implicitly. And that is the divine Author of Scripture, the Holy Spirit. Though the Bible is a compilation of writings from many men, they all had something significant in common. They were men who "spoke from God as they were carried along by the Holy Spirit" (2 Peter 1:21).

Scripture was not conceived or created *by* man's imaginings, but rather, it was communicated *through* man under the inspiration of the Holy Spirit.[1] Human authors were speaking what was given to them from God's Spirit, making Scripture the inerrant Word of God.

This is why Paul didn't say that only *some* parts of Scripture are inspired and authored by the Spirit. He said, "*All* Scripture is

God-breathed" (2 Timothy 3:16 NIV, emphasis added). Meaning, if the Bible listed the author's name alongside the title on the spine of the book, we would find "The Holy Bible // The Holy Spirit" there. No coauthors involved and no endorsers needed.

But the Holy Spirit did, and does, more than inspire and author Scripture. He also illuminates it for us today. Through every word He is "showing us truth, exposing our rebellion, correcting our mistakes, training us to live God's way. Through the Word we are put together and shaped up for the tasks God has for us" (2 Timothy 3:16–17 MESSAGE).

The Necessity of God's Word

I distinctly remember a conversation that took me aback when a friend of mine, who faithfully follows Jesus, very casually mentioned that she didn't read the Bible. She must have seen the surprise on my face because, before I could inquire why, she went on to explain that because she hears the Bible taught in church on Sunday, and because she experiences God's presence in nature during the week, she gets enough time with God. Her schedule doesn't allow for more than that, she concluded.

I hope that my shock at what my friend said doesn't sound arrogant, because I am super aware of how much more there is for me to discover about and encounter in God's Word. I've already told you about all the reasons I felt unfit to write about the Holy Spirit, and lack of knowledge was at the top of the list, despite having studied Scripture almost all my life. My kids are also a constant reminder about the vast depth and breadth of God's Word. I often have to answer their hard questions by saying, "You know, that's a really great question. Let's open the Bible and ask the Spirit to reveal the answer because I need to learn more about this too."

I can also very much identify with my friend saying she doesn't have time to read the Bible. Oh, I get that. But the problem is that the fruit I bear in a day that doesn't begin in the Word of God attests to the *real* truth, which is that I don't have time *not* to read my Bible. Without it, I am navigating my day in my humanity, and not opening myself up to the supernatural filling of God—to the hope and joy and strength and wisdom in His Word that I desperately need to do life in His power and likeness.

My need for daily empowering through God's Word reminds me of this prayer by an unknown author:

Dear Lord,
So far I've done all right.
I haven't gossiped,
haven't lost my temper,
haven't been greedy, grumpy, nasty, selfish, or overindulgent.
I'm really glad about that.

But in a few minutes, God,
I'm going to get out of bed.
And from then on,
I'm going to need a lot more help.[2]

The help we need comes through the Word and Spirit.

The Necessity of God's Word *and* Spirit

See, the thing we often overlook about the Word is that the Spirit is always present, available to illuminate the words of Scripture. They are both essential to the thriving Christian life.

"If you just read about the power of God, without the influence of Spirit, you say, 'Oh, God is powerful.' Without the influence of the Spirit, all that can do is make a superficial impression on the top of you, but when the Spirit of God is there, you read about the power, and there's access. The truth begins to shine. It begins to change you, and what happens is your heart develops courage."[3]

If we want more of God's Spirit, we need to spend more time in God's Word. And if we spend more time in God's Word, we avail ourselves to the activity of the Holy Spirit.

And if we want to better apply God's Word, we need the empowering of the Holy Spirit. We need to ask Him to enable what God's Word requires.

For example, when we are comforted by Scripture, that's the person of the Holy Spirit applying the living Word to our hurting hearts. When we are convicted by Scripture, that's the person of the Holy Spirit—our sanctifier—applying the living Word to our rebellious hearts. When we are strengthened by Scripture (yes, you know what I am about to say), that is the Holy Spirit—our strengthener—applying the living Word to our feeble hearts.

Here's another thing: If we want to better understand God's Word, we need the discernment of the Holy Spirit. We need to ask Him to illuminate what He alone inspired.

For example, when we read Scripture and a verse jumps off the page at us—maybe even a verse we've read before but we now see something new in it—that's the person of the Holy Spirit showing us exactly what He knows we need to read in that moment. It's why we can read the same verse a hundred times and have the Holy Spirit illuminate something new every single time. God's Word is inexhaustible.

The extent to which we know God's Word *and* Spirit to be vital is the extent to which our relationship with Jesus will be vibrant. Ultimately, the Holy Spirit awakens us to the beauty of Jesus in the Word of God.

He Gives Understanding

I'd be remiss if I didn't also mention this: The illumination of Scripture, by the power of the Holy Spirit, is available to all of us—from those of us who have spent so little time in God's Word that we can't find a single book in the Bible except Genesis without referring to the table of contents, to those of us who would win the Vacation Bible School contest for looking up a verse in Scripture the quickest. (I loved that game, not gonna lie.)

I know too many folks who are intimidated by the Bible or say they simply don't know where to start so they settle for letting it collect dust on the shelf.

> The Holy Spirit is the best Bible teacher out there!

But we are missing out by keeping it closed! God's Word is alive, it is full of power, and it does essential work in our hearts. Our task is to open it and ask the Holy Spirit to help us understand it and apply it as we study it. The Holy Spirit is the best Bible teacher out there!

We don't have to be biblical experts to enjoy it or glean truth from it. And when it can't be understood, because His ways are so much higher than ours (Isaiah 55:8–9), we can ask the Holy Spirit to help us believe it, even when we can't fathom it.

Paul writes, "How great are God's riches! How deep are his wisdom and knowledge! Who can explain his decisions? Who can understand his ways?" (Romans 11:33 GNT). Because God is infinite and we are finite, there will always be things in Scripture we won't grasp and can't explain. But really, who wants to worship a God whose ways we can completely ascertain? Would we still deem Him worthy of our worship? And when the enemy causes uncertainty to create doubt, we can ask the Holy Spirit to convince our hearts that the Gospel is true.

He Helps Us Apply It

Let's ask Him to give us an insatiable appetite to apply His Word—and to apply *all* of it. Because as much as our fallen nature would like to have the freedom to pick the parts we believe and apply, we don't have that freedom. I mean, I guess we *do* in the sense that we have free will, but we have nothing to gain and everything to lose by living that way.

Humility really behooves us here, because to say that we have the authority to choose which passages God wants us to honor and uphold is to question the sovereignty of God. And to choose to live outside the healthy guardrails God has established for us in His Word is to, like a bowling ball, end up in the gutters of life.

So let us approach Scripture with the same prayer as the psalmist who wrote, "Open my eyes that I may see wonderful things in your law" (Psalm 119:18 NIV). In that posture, we welcome the Holy Spirit to illuminate the words He alone inspired, and we can be sure He will show up to help us apply it.

last but not least

Reflect: Read 2 Timothy 3:14–17. Can you identify times you have experienced the Spirit equipping you for "every good work" through Scripture?

Respond: As you open Scripture in the days ahead, invite the Holy Spirit to illuminate the text and open your heart to the teaching, reproof, correction, and training in righteousness that make you complete.

eleven

He Empowered Jesus

We could file this chapter under the category "Things you might not want to confess when writing a book about the Holy Spirit," because I'm about to tell you something that might blow up any confidence you have in anything I write. Ready? I did not realize how dependent Jesus was on the power of the Holy Spirit for His ministry. This is such an exciting discovery because it simply affirms how we have no business trying to do anything—not a single thing—apart from the power of the Holy Spirit. We need Him, just as Jesus needed Him and just as the disciples needed Him.

Of course, we know that the Holy Spirit was intimately involved in the life of Jesus from the moment He was conceived by the power of the Holy Spirit in Mary's womb. But do we know the significance of the Holy Spirit equipping Jesus for ministry through His baptism by John?

> Then Jesus came from Galilee to the Jordan to be baptized by John. But John tried to deter him, saying, "I need to be baptized by you, and do you come to me?"
>
> Jesus replied, "Let it be so now; it is proper for us to do this to fulfill all righteousness." Then John consented.

> As soon as Jesus was baptized, he went up out of the water. At that moment heaven was opened, and he saw the Spirit of God descending like a dove and lighting on him.
>
> And a voice from heaven said, "This is my Son, whom I love; with him I am well pleased."

Matthew 3:13–17 NIV

When Jesus came up from the water, two striking things happened. First, the Spirit of God filled Him and empowered Him for His earthly ministry. Second, God the Father affirmed Jesus as His Son in whom He was well pleased.

God's affirmation of His love and pleasure in Jesus at His baptism demonstrates it wasn't performance-based. God wasn't pleased only after Jesus performed His miracles and wonders in the power of the Spirit. God wasn't pleased with Jesus only after He did not succumb to temptation by Satan in the wilderness in the very next passage. His sonship alone—as the sinless Son of God—made Jesus pleasing to God.

Are we seeing how freeing this is? This is how the Father now loves us because of Jesus. God's pleasure in us isn't performance-based. It's Jesus-based. So we can assuredly believe that because of Jesus, God speaks to our hearts, "You are my child, whom I love and with whom I am pleased . . . *because* you are covered in the righteousness of my Son."

The Dove Remained

All four Gospels attest to the baptism of Jesus, and though I took the above account from Matthew, I think it's worth noting what John wrote as well.

> Then John gave this testimony: "I saw the Spirit come down from heaven as a dove and remain on him."

John 1:32 NIV

By using the word *remain*, John reveals another essential piece of the story, which is the permanent relational presence between Jesus and the Holy Spirit. It was fascinating for me to learn about a dove's behavior, primarily their skittish ways. A dove would be quick to flee at any interruption to peace. But the dove feels right at home in Jesus' holiness and perfection. There is no interruption to peace in the person of Jesus.

Unlike our lives that can grieve the Holy Spirit, causing the dove's activity to diminish in our lives, the Holy Spirit's activity in Jesus' life would never be interrupted because there was no sin in Jesus. This means that Jesus' ministry was *continually* accomplished through the power of the Spirit.

Jesus' Ministry in the Power of the Spirit

After His baptism, "Jesus, *full of the Holy Spirit*, returned from the Jordan and was led by the Spirit in the wilderness for forty days, being tempted by the devil. And he ate nothing during those days. And when they were ended, he was hungry" (Luke 4:1–2, emphasis added).

Again, I'll confess that I'd heard this story a hundred times, but never noticed how the story opens by telling us how Jesus was "full of the Holy Spirit."

Think of all the foolish things we do and sins we succumb to when we're "hangry." Hunger makes us angry and weak and foolish. But not Jesus. In the wilderness, Jesus, though hungry and physically weak, was spiritually strong and without sin. Full of the power of the Holy Spirit, He experienced real temptation by Satan. He knows exactly how we feel when we are tempted to look at that thing, say that thing, drink that thing, use that thing, buy that thing, do that thing. Oh yes, Jesus knows temptation, but He never kneeled to it. Full of the Holy Spirit, and with the knowledge of the Old Testament Scriptures, Jesus used "the sword of the Spirit, which is the Word of God" (Ephesians 6:17) and defeated every attempt of Satan's. (Notice the Word and Spirit connection!)

We have the same power Jesus had to fight sin and defeat the enemy's temptation because we have the INpowering of the Holy Spirit and the sword of the Spirit.

What happens next?

Satan "departed from Him until an opportune time" (Luke 4:13). We need to see this! Satan is no quitter. Not with Jesus then, and not with us now. This is why we need the supernatural power of God through His Spirit and in His Word. Satan looks for "opportune times" to attack our minds with lies and bring destruction in our lives. Persistence is his specialty. When you ask, "Why do I keep struggling with these destructive behaviors or harmful beliefs about myself?" now you know. It's the enemy's determination to take you down. Your job is to walk in the victory already secured for you by Jesus.

> We have the same power Jesus had to fight sin and defeat the enemy's temptation because we have the INpowering of the Holy Spirit and the sword of the Spirit.

What happens next? It keeps getting better.

Jesus returned—in the power of the Holy Spirit—to Galilee to begin His ministry. Tested and proven faithful to His Father, Jesus gets to work.

He went to Nazareth, the town where He was raised, where He was given the scroll of Isaiah, and He proclaimed these holy words:

"The Spirit of the Lord is on me,
    because he has anointed me
    to proclaim good news to the poor.
He has sent me to proclaim freedom for the prisoners
    and recovery of sight for the blind,

to set the oppressed free,
to proclaim the year of the Lord's favor."

Then he rolled up the scroll, gave it back to the attendant and sat down. The eyes of everyone in the synagogue were fastened on him. He began by saying to them, "Today this scripture is fulfilled in your hearing."

Luke 4:18–21 NIV

Some of my favorite stories in the Bible are the ones where I can almost imagine Jesus doing a mic drop when He's done speaking because of how He leaves a crowd astonished by His teaching. This is one of those times.

Of course, He wouldn't drop the mic, because it's associated with boasting, but He certainly didn't mince words to make truth more digestible. Truth and love—that was His communication style.

Did the hearers like what Jesus had to say? Oh, they did not. They reacted with indignation, and that's putting it lightly. They were filled with wrath and drove Him out and tried to throw Him off a cliff. Literally. His ministry didn't seem to be starting off well, but this was not a surprise to Jesus. Nothing ever is. He knew He had come to be persecuted and die to pay the price of rebellion and sin for you and for me.

Where did His courage and conviction come from? How did He persevere under such harsh opposition? The power of the Holy Spirit.

And just like Jesus, we have the power of God's Spirit inside us and the power of God's Word to guide us! Through every trial and temptation we face, we already have the victory. That should get us pretty fired up.

It should also make us wonder why we would ever pass up such power by neglecting His presence in our lives.

> Through every trial and temptation we face, we already have the victory.

Wait!

In John 14:15–31, we find what is probably Jesus' most significant teaching on the Trinity. In this passage, Jesus promises the power of the Holy Spirit to His disciples—power that will literally change *everything* for them. See, Jesus knows His death is imminent, so He begins preparing His disciples for the work of the Holy Spirit in *their* lives. He assures them that the same supernatural power and help they've witnessed the Spirit giving Him will soon be given to them.

Now fast-forward to when the resurrected Jesus (who just endured the cross, defeated death, and rose from the grave) briefly appeared to His disciples with the greeting "Peace to you." He enjoyed a meal with them, He reminded them they were witnesses to Him fulfilling everything that was written about Him, and then He concludes with this important instruction (my paraphrase): "Stay! Wait for the Spirit's power!"

Jesus said, "And now I will send the Holy Spirit, just as my Father promised. But stay here in the city until the Holy Spirit comes and fills you with power from heaven" (Luke 24:49 NLT).

The last recorded instructions of Christ in the gospel of Luke—before He was taken up into heaven—were Jesus telling His disciples, "Don't even *think* about trying to do the work of the Father without the power of the Spirit."

Do we see the pattern? Jesus waited until He was empowered with the Holy Spirit to begin His earthly ministry, and Jesus told the disciples to wait until after they had the power of the Holy Spirit to begin their ministry. This pattern is passed down to us today.

Just after Jesus instructs His disciples to wait to witness until they've received God's power, He

> led them out to the vicinity of Bethany, he lifted up his hands and blessed them. While he was blessing them, he left them and was

taken up into heaven. Then they worshiped him and returned to Jerusalem with great joy. And they stayed continually at the temple, praising God.

Luke 24:50–53 NIV

This concludes the gospel of Luke, and what happens next, at Pentecost, is in the book of Acts. The story just keeps getting better, so keep reading to see the dramatic difference it made for the disciples.

last but not least

Reflect: Have you ever found yourself struggling with destructive behaviors or harmful beliefs about yourself? Name them quietly in your heart or consider writing them down.

Respond: The enemy wants nothing more than to hold you hostage to those things you've named. Friend, hand them over to the Holy Spirit today and claim the victory over them in Jesus' name. Practice this daily, or hourly. By the power of the Holy Spirit, walk in victory over the enemy's schemes today!

twelve

He Gave Power
to the Disciples

Mike and I have been part of the same couple's Bible study for about six years. Oh, how I love this tribe. Every other Friday night we gather with about eight other couples to enjoy a delicious meal and study God's Word, and it's always the highlight of my weekend.

Last year our group studied the book of Acts and we had the most incredible discussions around our shared awe of all that the Holy Spirit accomplished *through* people who simply made themselves available for His power to be activated in their lives.

This revelation led me to grapple with the question, "Am I available?" because there isn't anything the Holy Spirit did through the disciples that He isn't still fully capable of doing today through men and women who wholeheartedly say, "I am available!"

The Disciples Waited

Luke opens the book of Acts with a refresher on how Jesus promised the coming of the Holy Spirit to the disciples. Jesus specifically said two things would happen: They would be baptized with the Holy Spirit (Acts 1:5) and, as a result, they would receive power to witness to the ends of the earth (Acts 1:8).

But remember, Jesus didn't tell them when the Holy Spirit would descend. They wouldn't know the time. They wouldn't know the date. They would simply have to wait, which for most of us is about as fun as getting a root canal and as easy as climbing Mount Everest.

After giving these instructions, Jesus departs in a rather dramatic fashion. "He was taken up before their very eyes, and a cloud hid him from their sight'" (Acts 1:1–2, 9 NIV).

I guess that when someone not only defeats the grave but is then taken up in a cloud before your very eyes, you heed their instructions, because the disciples did just as Jesus said! But as we know, this hasn't always been the case. They weren't always the most dependable crew. But this time they listened. They waited.

The Waiting Room

Several years ago my speaking schedule ramped up and I was traveling quite a bit to speak at various events around the country. But about six months into my busy schedule, the peace I needed to have before saying yes to a speaking request began to wane. In fact, I no longer had any peace about traveling and speaking at the same pace. My first question to God was, "Did I do something wrong? Why, when I pray about these invitations, can I not get any peace about accepting? Why aren't you sending me out?" I mistook His protection for punishment.

God knew a complex season was ahead for my family. And He knew that my utmost desire was to serve and love my family well. He knew my husband would need to work especially hard to lead his company well in that season, our four boys would walk through various challenges that needed their mom fully present, our family would experience a heartbreaking situation with a foster child, and we would begin the process of welcoming Andre, our fifth son, into our family. God knew that my mom, who is usually available to love on our kids while I travel, would become ill and would need to remain home with my dad.

God wanted me to wait because more than ever, my main mission field was in my home. It was also during this season that God wanted to draw me deeper into relationship with Him. It was during this time that I was given the bandwidth to completely immerse myself in the study of His Spirit. Thank God I waited. But you should know, waiting doesn't come easy to me.

Said differently, I haven't always waited when I knew that was what God was asking me to do. In fact, some of the worst decisions of my life have been made when I've busted out of the waiting room before God said "Go."

Maybe you can relate? When we have good work we want to do, or ideas we believe will benefit the kingdom, or dreams we want to see come to fruition, waiting can feel like a waste of time.

But experience, and a little maturity, have taught me that when I pray and I don't get peace to say yes to the invitation in front of me or take the next step into an opportunity that beckons me, I need to wait. Yes, I've learned that His plans are always better than ours, and His power is the necessary fuel. The sooner we learn to trust Him and wait on His timing, the better off we'll be.

I can't help but wonder, what if the disciples hadn't waited on God to fulfill His promise to send His Spirit? What if, in eagerness to share the Gospel and do good work, they began to teach in their own wisdom and strength?

What if?

Not only did they wait, but I love that Luke included in his writing the posture they took while they waited. I have so much to learn from the way they waited. In the waiting, he wrote, "They praised God with great joy." Their posture was praise, and their prize was power. Wow.

The power the disciples needed back then is the same power we need now. We *need* the Holy Spirit to do the holy work of God.

And the holy work of God isn't just a stage or a microphone or a platform. The holy work of God is every single small moment of our everyday lives. It's how we love our neighbor, our husband, our children, our friends, and our enemies.

The holy work of God is being faithful to shine His light in the places He has put us—under our roofs and in our workplaces, in orphanages in other countries, and in the coffee shop down the street. The holy work of God is pointing people to the love of Jesus. And to do that the way God designed, we need—we cannot do without—the power of His Spirit.

And here's the sweet relief: Because of Pentecost, we don't have to!

The Feast of Pentecost

Pentecost was the day the Father fulfilled His promise to pour out the Holy Spirit not just *onto* but *into* His people. It occurred ten days after Jesus' ascension into heaven. At 9 a.m., the Holy Spirit was unleashed in the Upper Room into 120 people, including the disciples, and each one received the supernatural power of God that forever changed how we get to experience God's power now. It is a power that continues to defy human understanding and supersede human strength.

The story unfolded in the most dramatic way. A bunch of Jesus' friends were waiting in a room together when the sound of a mighty wind blew in from heaven. And then they all saw what appeared to be blasts of fire flickering over one another's heads. In this moment, they were all filled with the Holy Spirit and they began to speak in other tongues (Acts 2:1–4), thus fulfilling John the Baptist's prophecy that Jesus would pour out His Spirit on His people.

We know what wind sounds like. We know what fire looks like. But what does Luke mean when He writes that they began to "speak in other tongues as the Spirit enabled them?" (Acts 2:4 NIV).

It means they were each empowered to speak other known and recognizable languages they had not personally known how to speak previously. The glorious thing happening here—that is often overlooked but is so crucial to the story—is that the Gospel was no longer confined to the Hebrew language.

God was so intentional in His timing! Check this out: The Holy Spirit descended on a day that devout Jews from every nation under heaven annually gather in Jerusalem. And when the God-fearing Jews heard the commotion in the Upper Room, they came running to see what was happening. In doing so, they were all able to hear the Gospel being preached in their own language and bore witness to the mighty work of the Holy Spirit.

The disciples couldn't have seen this coming. They were just a bunch of ordinary Jesus-loving guys who were gathered in a room with no real plan. But the Holy Spirit had a plan and He gave them the power to fulfill that plan.

The good news of salvation in Jesus was now accessible to every nation and language. God ordained it, and the Holy Spirit enabled it! But not everyone who bore witness to it believed it or liked it. (Sounds a lot like our world today.)

Pentecost was such a joyous and historic moment that those who bore witness to it were amazed and perplexed, and some even accused the 120 of being drunk on wine because of their behavior. But the 120 weren't overcome by wine, they were overcome with the Spirit of God Almighty. They were high on the Holy Spirit.

Long, long ago, God gave power to His disciples, and He's still in the business of empowering His children today. You may have never had a visible tongue of fire flickering over your sweet head, sister, but His power is all over you. Believe it.

He Is a Person, Not a Power

In closing, I want to highlight an important lesson we can glean from the disciples after Pentecost: The Holy Spirit isn't a power for people to wield. He is a Person who manifests His power in the people of God who make themselves available. The disciples were merely conduits of God's power. And they always gave God the praise for what they accomplished in His name.

Let me tell you a quick but great story from Acts 8:9–23 (NLT) to illustrate this.

A man by the name of Simon (often called Simon the Magician) was a well-known sorcerer who astounded the people of Samaria with his magic tricks. But when Philip the disciple came onto the scene in Samaria, preaching the good news of Jesus in the power of the Holy Spirit, Simon, along with many men and women of Samaria, repented and were baptized.

When Peter and John heard this news, they traveled from Jerusalem to Samaria to lay their hands on the new believers and pray for them to receive the Holy Spirit.

When Simon saw that the Spirit was given when the apostles laid their hands on people, he offered them money to buy this power. "Let me have this power, too," he exclaimed, "so that when I lay my hands on people, they will receive the Holy Spirit!" (v. 19).

In response, Peter strongly rebuked him and told him to repent for treating God's Spirit like a commodity that could be bought for personal benefit and fame.

> Do you know what a priceless treasure lives in you?

Simon's story shows us that the Holy Spirit's blessing won't be bought. His power can't be purchased. He is a priceless gift given to everyone who puts their trust in Jesus. Do you know what a priceless treasure lives in you? No amount of worldly wealth can purchase the gift of the Spirit's transforming power. Repentance and faith are the only way.

Simon's story also reminds us that having the Holy Spirit's power is never about our own fame but for the fame of God's name, so that others will see what is only possible with God. God gives us His power—as we live out our purpose—for the praise of His name!

Nobody knew this better than Peter. Let's look at his incredible story in the next chapter.

last but not least

Reflect: Read Acts 2:12. Think about a time when you were amazed or perplexed by something that happened in your life that could only be explained by the supernatural power of the Holy Spirit. It could be something small or something big. And if you're struggling to identify where the Spirit's power has manifested in your life, sit with the question, "Am I available?"

Respond: Ask the Holy Spirit to make you hungry for His power to be manifested in your life in a way that makes others wonder, "What does this mean?" and "Where does this power come from?" so you have an opportunity to point them to the person of Jesus.

thirteen

He Gave Power to Peter

A popular birthday gift among our boys and their friends is gift cards. Their favorites are Amazon and Xbox. To me, it feels so . . . unthoughtful, but this is not a hill I will die on. But here's the thing about gift cards: Even when you have the card in your possession, freely given to you as a gift, it does you no good until it's activated. You don't benefit from it until you activate it.

Similarly, we can have in our possession a valuable—priceless, actually—gift. The power of the Holy Spirit. The same power witnessed at Pentecost is available to us today. But if it's never activated, we deny ourselves the benefits. Because having access to the Spirit doesn't equate to experiencing His activity. What a tragedy for the believer.

But unlike a gift card, for which we submit a code to activate its spending power, God activates His supernatural power in us when we yield to His Spirit.

Peter's life is a prime example of how the activity of the Holy Spirit can alter our lives. When God's power was activated in Peter, the transformation was so undeniable and remarkable that it's worth taking a look at his incredible story and seeing how it can inspire ours.

Peter's Legendary Sermon

Picking up where we left off, the 120 have just been accused of day drinking—or actually 9 a.m. drinking—but rather than cower at the criticism and pressure of the opposition (something Peter knew much about prior to Pentecost!), Peter had a newfound confidence and boldness to witness.

Now empowered by the Holy Spirit, Peter lifted his voice and preached a legendary sermon about salvation being available to all men and women, both Jew and Gentile, young and old.

What you see was predicted long ago by the prophet Joel:

"In the last days," God says,
   "I will pour out my Spirit upon all people.
Your sons and daughters will prophesy.
   Your young men will see visions,
      and your old men will dream dreams. . . .
But everyone who calls on the name of the LORD
   will be saved"

Acts 2:16–17, 21 NLT

This monumental moment had been predicted by the prophet Joel six hundred years prior. The formerly fearful Peter was now reciting Old Testament passages about Jesus pouring out His Spirit on all people.

"Exalted to the right hand of God," Peter concludes, "[Jesus] has received from the Father the promised Holy Spirit and has poured out what you now see and hear. . . . Let all Israel be assured of this: God has made this Jesus, whom you crucified, both Lord and Christ" (Acts 2:33, 36 NIV).

I can only imagine the passion with which he preached! His words so bold: "Be assured of this!"

Having just watched *The Passion of the Christ* with my family—something we do every Easter—I'm freshly reminded just how unforgiving and hostile the opposition to Jesus was, and how gutsy it was of Peter to declare salvation in Jesus. Only and all made possible by the power of the Spirit.

Pre-Pentecost Peter

To truly appreciate Peter's boldness, we need to remember who "pre-Pentecost" Peter was, *before* the indwelling Holy Spirit gave Him supernatural power.

Honestly, I just love that it's Peter, of all people, who preaches, because his track record was wrought with failure. From the moment Jesus called this fisherman to follow Him, to the unfolding of his disloyalty at Jesus' crucifixion, Peter struggled to faithfully trust and follow Jesus.

I am so tempted to tell every fascinating detail of Peter's life story because who he is post-Pentecost stands in such stark contrast to who he was. But I'll skip to what happened just before Jesus' crucifixion. Maybe you know the story.

Just after Jesus was arrested and headed to the cross, a young servant girl accused Peter of being associated with Jesus, but Peter denied knowing His Lord. This is the same Peter who went on to deny knowing Jesus two more times within the hour. This is the same Peter who cared deeply about the opinions of others and was labeled a coward for denying Jesus. He later wept bitterly at his disloyalty, revealing his genuine love for Jesus. See, Peter didn't lack love for the Son of God. He lacked the power of the Spirit of God.

> Peter didn't lack love for the Son of God. He lacked the power of the Spirit of God.

Peter's story gives me a lot of hope for my own.

Post-Pentecost Peter is now utterly fearless in proclaiming the name of Christ in the face of adversity. His life is the prime ex-

ample of the radical change that occurs in a person who has en-
countered the grace and Spirit of God.

See, I think both those things are at play here: grace and power.
After the resurrection, Peter was restored to relationship with
Jesus. Over breakfast, by the fire, Jesus gives Peter the invitation
to affirm his love for Him. For each of his three denials of Jesus
before His crucifixion, Jesus asked him, "Do you love me?" And
each time that Peter says, "I do," Jesus commissions him to feed His
sheep. In other words, Jesus is saying, "Out of love for me, go forth
caring about what I care about: my sheep." (See John 21:15–17.)

Jesus not only forgave Peter, but He reinstated him. And here
is the best part. Did you notice how Jesus didn't ask him, "Can
I trust you not to fail me again?" He asked, "*Do you love me?*"
Jesus actually knew Peter would falter again. But it's never been
about our behavior with Jesus. Jesus, above all, wants our love.
Faithfulness will flow from love that is empowered by the Spirit.

Jesus prioritizes having our hearts over having our effort. As
demonstrated through Peter, He doesn't forgive us and commission us based on our promise to have better behavior. He restores
us out of His impossible-to-grasp grace.

Grace is at play in Peter's desire to unabashedly preach the
Gospel. That's the first thing. And the second thing at play is the
transforming power of God's Spirit.

Cut to the Heart

Peter's transformation was so attractive, and his sermon so
powerful, that the crowd was "cut to the heart" (Acts 2:37 NIV)
and they asked, "What shall we do" to have this too? They wanted
whatever it was that Peter had.

Peter answered their curiosity boldly: "Repent and be baptized,
and the Holy Spirit will be yours too." (See Acts 2:38.)[1]

Peter's next words are a soothing balm for anyone who worries
they aren't worthy of God's indwelling presence. "The promise

is for you and your children and for all who are *far off*—for all whom the Lord our God will call" (v. 39 NIV, emphasis added).

Are you afraid you're too far off? This promise is for you. It's for me. There are no exceptions to this promise. None of us has rebelled too much or run too far.

None of us has rebelled too much or run too far.

On that day, three thousand people accepted Peter's message. But the disciples were just getting started! So many extraordinary stories were about to unfold.

One such story goes like this: When Peter and John were headed to the temple to pray, they passed through the temple gate where there was a crippled beggar who asked them for money. Rather than give him money, Peter completely healed him in the name of Jesus Christ. The man, who was recognizable to all the onlookers because he often sat at the gate begging, then "went with them into the temple courts, walking and jumping, and praising God" (Acts 3:8 NIV).

As people gathered in amazement at the healed beggar, Peter seized the opportunity to preach the Gospel. "People of Israel," he said, "what is so surprising about this? And why stare at us as though we had made this man walk by our own power or godliness?" (Acts 3:12 NLT). "By faith in the name of Jesus, this man who you see and know was made strong" (Acts 3:16 NIV).

Peter uses this display of power to point to Jesus and assures the crowd that none of his miraculous works are because of his own power or godliness. Pointing people to Jesus, and only Jesus, is his aim.

> When they saw the courage of Peter and John and realized that they were unschooled, ordinary men, they were astonished.
>
> Acts 4:13 NIV

Meanwhile, Peter and the apostles continued to preach Jesus and work miracles in His name. "More and more men and women

106

believed in the Lord and were added to their number. As a result, people brought the sick into the streets and laid them on beds and mats so that at least Peter's shadow might fall on some of them as he passed by" (Acts 5:14–15 NIV). Yes, Peter's mere shadow was sought after!

Extraordinary Power in an Ordinary Life

What's happening here?

Peter and John were ordinary men, but they had the extraordinary power of the Holy Spirit. And how they lived their life made the power of the Spirit irresistible to those who witnessed it.

It makes me wonder, *Does my ordinary life testify to the extraordinary power of God? Is my life a signpost for Jesus? Does my life make the power of the Holy Spirit undeniable and irresistible? I may not be healing lame beggars at the temple gate, but does my life exhibit the miraculous fruit only the Holy Spirit can produce?*

Maybe we should sit with these questions for a bit. What would need to change in our inner lives for our outer lives to be so profoundly influential for the Gospel?

"Peter's testimony is exhibit A of the power of the Holy Spirit to transform weakness into strength, fearfulness into courage, timidity into boldness, impulsiveness into self-control, foolishness into wisdom, and a pattern of failure into resounding eternal success," writes Ann Graham Lotz.[2]

> What would need to change in our inner lives for our outer lives to be so profoundly influential for the Gospel?

Peter's transformation was the supernatural work of the Spirit. And we can experience that too. You've been given the gift of the Holy Spirit. Will you neglect it or ask God to activate it?

Our willingness + His power = supernatural outcomes.

107

last but not least

Reflect: In what area of your life do you need the Holy Spirit to transform weakness into strength, or a pattern of failure into a testimony of victory?

Respond: Yield yourself to the Holy Spirit's authority and invite Him to activate His power in the areas of your life where you need Him to work supernaturally. As He answers that prayer, always make it your aim to direct people's gaze to the God who saves.

fourteen

He Gives Power to Us

Candace Cameron Bure created a T-shirt that reads "INpowered Woman: A woman who derives her strength from God's limitless power within her" (see Philippians 4:13). How good is that? I'm borrowing her term "INpowered" for our conversation because I love how it reminds us that God's power is more than an outside force. His power indwells us. We're more than empowered women. We are INpowered by God himself.

As Christians, we are set free from striving to be the superheroes of our stories! We are liberated from relying on our own inner strength, which in reality isn't all that impressive, but it *is* super exhausting. Can we just admit that together? Our inner strength— apart from God's inner strengthening—isn't much to brag about. But there's a good reason for that. God didn't design us to do *anything* apart from His Spirit. So if we buy in to the messaging that we can mantra up whatever it is that we need to navigate the struggles of this life, we forego witnessing what's only possible with the Spirit. What a travesty that would be.

How to Live by the Power of the Spirit

Knowing we *have* God's power is different from knowing how to *live* by God's power, and I think this is where a lot of us struggle.

I don't think most Christians avoid living by the power of the Holy Spirit intentionally. I just think He seems inaccessible to a lot of us, and the actual ability to draw on His power feels unattainable. But whatever the reason, we too often neglect to take hold of the benefits of the divine *Person* who resides inside us.

Now is a good time to change that storyline, so let's dive in to see how Scripture guides us in actually *living* by God's Spirit. Paul writes,

> Let me ask you this one question: Did you receive the Holy Spirit by obeying the law of Moses? Of course not! You received the Spirit because you believed the message you heard about Christist. . . .
>
> I ask you again, does God give you the Holy Spirit and work miracles among you because you obey the law? Of course not! It is because you believe the message you heard about Christ.
>
> Galatians 3:2, 5 NLT

Notice how Paul answers each question by emphasizing belief in the "message you heard about Jesus."

What Paul is showing us is that we *live* by the power of the Holy Spirit in the same way we first *received* the power of the Holy Spirit: by believing the message of Jesus Christ—the Gospel! And in case we aren't clear, Paul asks:

> How foolish can you be? After starting your new lives in the Spirit, why are you now trying to become perfect by your own human effort?
>
> Galatians 3:3 NLT

The Spirit sparks—and sustains—our new life in Christ. It is His work alone to activate the supernatural power of God in our lives. But . . . this doesn't mean we do nothing.

For Him to activate His power in our lives, we have to submit our lives to the way of Jesus. We have to surrender our wills to His, to say, "All I am and all I have is yours to use." And this has to be more than lip service. For God's power to be fully active in our lives, we have to be fully in with Him.

This is why we need to consider changing our question from, "How can I live in the Spirit's power?" to "How can I live more fully surrendered?"

> We have all of Him, but does He have all of us?

We have all of Him, but does He have all of us? When we don't submit, we settle for lives that don't bear witness to Christ as they could, and for lives that don't bear fruit as they should. Settling is what we do when we operate in our natural power rather than in the Spirit's supernatural power.

Trust or Fear?

Mike and I were in an unusually hectic season in life as I wrote this book. A hectic existence is something we intentionally fight against, but in a family of seven with five very active boys who range from four to twenty-four, a measure of (beautiful) chaos is inevitably woven into the narrative. Throw in a pandemic-induced quarantine and distance learning and you've got yourself a very full platter.

Overwhelmed is the best word I can use to describe how I felt in that season, and yet that word doesn't seem to do it justice. Some of the demands in front of us were good things with multiple details that needed to be worked out, and some of the demands were not good things, with details that only God could work out in hearts in our home, but I began to treat it all as one big burden because of how overwhelmed I felt. I can see now that I just wanted to eliminate things from our plate because I was functioning from a place of fear.

My perspective shift came one evening when I was settled into the couch on the outdoor patio while Mike was chipping golf balls into the net he set up in our backyard. While we talked through everything on our plate, I stopped mid-sentence and blurted out that I just couldn't handle it all. "There is just too much to do. I can't do everything that needs to be done. I can't solve everything that needs to be solved. I can't do it all, at least not well." Mike turned his head toward me from across the yard. He didn't say anything; he didn't need to. I heard the words I spoke, and I was challenged in my core to change the dialogue from "There is too much that needs to be done. I can't do it all" to "I can't but He can. I will trust God to do what only He can do. I will trust God to INpower me by His Spirit."

I had to make a choice. Choose to trust that the Spirit would supply, or function from a place of fear.

As He always does, God provided what was needed in that season. Wisdom was imparted. Deadlines were moved without my asking. Joy was let loose. Children repented. Provision was given. I don't mean for this to sound like all the outcomes were tied up with a pretty bow, because they weren't. My heart still broke over things I couldn't fix, my head still swirled with things out of my control, and many nights I lay restless in bed, my only relief the prayers that ushered me back to sleep. But we witnessed God working where we could not, and we experienced His inner strengthening by His Spirit. And that is the good stuff. The best stuff.

Making Him Feel Welcome

Just as Jesus was home to the Holy Spirit during His earthly ministry, so too are you home to the Holy Spirit now. I mean, think about that. That's crazy! We have the same Helper Jesus had when He was tempted to sin by Satan and didn't succumb. We have the same Helper Jesus had when He defeated death. We have the same unstoppable Spirit of God living inside us!

So maybe a good follow-up question to "How can I live by the power of the Holy Spirit?" is "How can I make Him feel more welcome in His own home?" Because *you* are His home. *You* are the temple of the Holy Spirit. (I've given us the opportunity to wrestle with this, in depth, in the "Last but Not Least" section at the end of this chapter.)

To be honest, I wish there were a checklist for living in the power of the Holy Spirit, because then it would feel like I had more control over how He works in my life. Ah, there it is—the truth I didn't realize until it passed from my fingertips to my keyboard just now. Ouch. I want to control the Holy Spirit's work in my life. I want to know that if I check boxes A, B, C, and D, it means I am living by His power. But that's not how our *relational* God works. He says, "Spend time with me, store my living Word in you, and make your heart a welcoming home for my Spirit."

Think about this: How much energy do we put into making sure our homes are decorated and cleaned so our family and friends experience it as a loving, welcoming, and enjoyable space? This is why my favorite show is still *Fixer Upper*, even though I have to settle for reruns now. I love learning ways to make my home be the best it can be. But do I feel the same way about making the Holy Spirit's home the best it can be? That convicts me good.

Ask for It

Finally, if we want to live by His power, Jesus says, "Ask for it!" But this isn't a one and done. Jesus says, "Keep on asking, and you will receive what you ask for. Keep on seeking, and you will find. Keep on knocking, and the door will be opened to you" (Luke 11:9–10 NLT).

And then Jesus drives home the point by comparing the good gifts we want to give our kids with how much more God longs to answer our persistent prayers.

"You fathers—if your children ask for a fish, do you give them a snake instead? Or if they ask for an egg, do you give them a scorpion? Of course not! So if you sinful people know how to give good gifts to your children, how much more will your heavenly Father give the Holy Spirit to those who ask him" (Luke 11:11–13 NLT).

Ask Him to fill you with His Spirit, over and over and over again. And then walk according to it. There is no limit to what God can do in and through a life surrendered to and empowered by His Spirit.

last but not least

Reflect: How can I make the Holy Spirit feel more welcome in His own home inside me?

Respond: I mentioned that we'd be doing a little extra reflection today. Let's do a Holy Spirit inventory together and answer the following questions as honestly as we can:

Am I grieving Him by living in intentional sin, or am I seeking first the face of God?

Am I filling my life with His living Word, or am I trying to satisfy my soul with the things of this world?

Am I repenting for my rebellion and receiving the unceasing forgiveness given to me in Jesus, or am I asking the Holy Spirit to co-exist with unrepentance?

As you answer these questions, remember this isn't about being perfect for Christ—not even close. This is about being in pursuit of Christ! With our eyes fixed on Jesus, the Spirit settles ungrieved in our souls, and His power is unleashed in our lives!

Spend time sitting in the Spirit's presence, allowing Him to bring to mind areas in your life that you have not surrendered. Then confess those things to the Lord and receive the assurance that your sins are forgiven. Stand in the confidence that the Spirit will manifest His power in your life.

fifteen

He Is the Spirit of Truth

If you were taught to memorize Scripture as a child, or if it's something you've learned to cherish later in life, I'm going to guess that one of the verses stored in your heart is John 14:6, where Jesus said, "I am the way and the truth and the life. No one comes to the Father except through me" (NIV).

In this well-known verse, Jesus is teaching the disciples that the only way we receive eternal life with God the Father is through belief in Him as God the Son. He is the way. He is the truth. He is the life.

What I find so fascinating is that soon thereafter, Jesus uses this word *truth* again when speaking about the Spirit. One such example is found in John 16:13: "When the Spirit of truth comes, he will guide you into all the truth, for he will not speak on his own authority, but whatever he hears he will speak, and he will declare to you the things that are to come."

Just like Jesus, the Holy Spirit is characterized by truth. He opens our hearts to the truth of Christ and goes on illuminating truth to us in Scripture. Without the Spirit of truth working in our life, we will never know the Truth, Jesus Christ. This is what Paul meant when He wrote, "The person without the Spirit does not accept the things that come from the Spirit of God but considers them foolishness, and cannot understand them because they are discerned only through the Spirit. . . . But we have the mind of Christ" (1 Corinthians 2:14, 16 NIV).

> Without the Spirit of truth working in our life, we will never know the Truth, Jesus Christ.

He Leads Us to Truth

Do you ever get discouraged or frustrated when you share the Gospel with someone and they seem to carelessly dismiss it or even belittle you for believing it? What Jesus is reminding us here is that the way the Spirit works and manifests in our lives is *supposed* to seem foolish to those who don't have the Spirit. We shouldn't be surprised when people who don't have the Holy Spirit are critical or skeptical. We cannot convince them of His beauty and purpose. We can only let them witness the beauty and benefits of Him in our own lives and pray their hearts will be opened to Him.

For example, I have a friend who—in the past—hasn't been afraid to tell me that she believes science disproves the salvation narrative, but more than that, she's afraid of what saying yes to Jesus will cost her. But in our last conversation, she said she keeps ending up in situations where it feels like God is "doing something" because she has a new and unexpected openness to faith. The last situation was one in which she was put on the spot to pray for a person who was in a desperate condition, and rather than resist, which is what she usually would have done, she prayed.

When she shared this story, I couldn't help but smile because it was evident the Holy Spirit was wooing her heart to a relationship with Jesus, which she has always said is "fine for you" but "not for me."

But it didn't surprise me because this is what the Spirit delights to do! He loves to lead us to truth! Is there someone in your life who has been resistant to the Gospel? A child? A neighbor? A sibling or a parent? Don't give up hope. Keep asking the Spirit of truth to lead them to the *Truth*.

> The Holy Spirit is an incredible leader.

The Holy Spirit is an incredible Leader and can be trusted to guide them there!

I love how Paul concludes the 1 Corinthians 2 passage on the Spirit with, "But we have the mind of Christ." What an extraordinary benefit to having the Spirit. I can barely fathom it. What occupies the mind of Christ can occupy our minds too. When I think about all the chaos and commotion that rattles around in my mind, keeping me anxious and agitated, I'm convicted to invite the Spirit to infuse my mind with the complete peace of Christ and give me thoughts that mimic His.

He Guides Us in Truth

Before the COVID-19 pandemic hit, I was secretly planning a trip to Israel for my husband's fiftieth birthday. I traveled to Israel several times when I was a child, as my parents led countless tours through the Holy Land back in the day, but Mike has never been, and I was so eager for us to experience it together.

I have vivid memories of floating in the Dead Sea with black mud slathered on my arms and legs, holding on to my dad for dear life while riding a rebellious camel, and touching the place where it's said Christ was born. I recall how surreal it felt to stand in the empty tomb and how, even as a child, I knew I was on holy ground.

I unfortunately had to put the trip on hold due to the pandemic, but when I thought we still had a shot at going, I asked several friends for recommendations of good tour guides, because experiences like that hinge on who is guiding you. You can go it alone and figure it out on the fly (encountering unnecessary frustration and wasting a lot of time), or you can let a knowledgeable and trustworthy guide lead the way.

I think the same can be said about life. We can go it alone or we can go with a guide—a top-rated guide, at that. This is, of course, the Holy Spirit, and while He doesn't cost us financially, allowing Him to be our guide does cost us our pride—as in the case of my friend being wooed by the Holy Spirit, who will have to humble herself and confess what she needs. It's what we all need. Holy help.

He Feeds Our Minds with the Good News

Have you ever endured a meal with a person who thought they knew everything about everything? "Check, please!" You can't eat fast enough because the whole meal is about feeding their ego. Well, the Holy Spirit actually *does* know everything about everything. And His whole goal is feeding you the Gospel. He testifies about Jesus (John 15:26).

Let's not let this get lost on us, because at the same time, we have an enemy—an aggressive and persistent enemy—who is committed to the exact opposite of the Holy Spirit. He is the ultimate deceiver.

Jesus didn't hold back when He spoke about Satan just a few chapters earlier in John 8:44: "He was a murderer from the beginning, and does not stand in the truth, because there is no truth in him. When he lies, he speaks out of his own character, for he is a liar and the father of lies."

I can only imagine the conviction with which Jesus spoke as He described the father of lies. I sense His holy anger over the enemy's goal to make us believe we are too far gone for the Gospel to rescue us. Or worse, that we're too good to need rescuing.

Without the Spirit, we stay entangled in the enemy's web of lies that keeps us from a free and flourishing life. This is why we need

119

the Spirit of truth. The Spirit's goal is to guide us to the Gospel—the good news that Jesus' perfect life, death, and resurrection have secured God's unwavering love for us, acceptance of us, delight in us, and pleasure over us.

Our all-knowing Helper guides us into the truth of *who God says we are* when we have put our trust in "the way and the truth and the life." He wants us to have confidence in our identity as a treasured, cherished, loved-with-no-conditions child of God. This is a great gift for those of us who tend to listen to the lies of the merciless critic.

He Brings Truth to Remembrance

Another priceless benefit to having the Spirit of truth is that He brings truth to remembrance when we need it most.

When Jesus told His disciples that the Holy Spirit will "teach you everything and remind you of everything I have told you" (John 14:26 NLT), I'm guessing the disciples were worried about not being able to recall and recite everything they needed to say when it was their time to spread the Gospel. As we often do, they were probably thinking only in terms of what they could accomplish on their own. They were relying on natural recollection rather than supernatural, Spirit-empowered recollection.

But the Spirit was going to help them recall everything they needed to remember. From Old Testament prophecy to the very words they witnessed spoken from the mouth of their Master, the Spirit would bring it to memory. The New Testament bears witness to the fulfillment of this promise.

Likewise, the Holy Spirit will help *us* recall what we have read and studied in Scripture. He will bring to memory what has *already* been stored inside us. That being said, the Holy Spirit can't remind us of things we don't know. This is why we need to be steeped in the Word.

The Holy Spirit reminding the disciples of everything Jesus said to them was essential for the flourishing of the church and the writing of the New Testament. And the Holy Spirit reminding *us* of everything in Scripture is essential for our witness today.

Can you think of times when the Holy Spirit has brought to memory the truth of Scripture?

I've shed some thankful tears as I've reflected on how this gift of the Spirit has been active in my life—for how He's stirred up Scripture in my heart and mind when I've needed it most. In heartbreak to comfort me. In a fight against sin to empower me. When I've needed to tell shame it can no longer stake claim in my heart.

When my kids have needed correction, He brings to memory a verse for training their hearts in godliness, *or* when my boys need affirmation of their sonship in Jesus (because Scripture was never meant to be just for correction), He brings to memory a verse that speaks of God's unconditional welcome of them.

> The Holy Spirit brings to mind the promises of God we've deposited in the storehouses of our hearts.

When speaking from a stage with a mic in my hand, and when I've been speaking on the phone with a friend who needed a word of encouragement, the Holy Spirit has been helping me recall truth stored in my heart.

The Holy Spirit brings to mind the promises of God we've deposited in the storehouses of our hearts. But He needs material to work with, so let's give it to Him. With a storehouse filled with the Word of God, we will never be powerless in fighting sin, never lacking an inspired word to share with a friend, and always able to ruminate on the truth that brings life and peace to our minds.

Where He guides, you can confidently go. He will never mislead you or guide you outside God's will. He will never get you lost or bring you to a spot where you need to make a U-turn. He is completely trustworthy and faithful. He is always guiding you straight to life-giving truth.

last but not least

Reflect: Has the Holy Spirit ever brought to mind a promise from Scripture that was stored in your heart and that you needed during an especially challenging time? What difference did that Scripture make in your situation?

Respond: The Bible emphasizes the benefits of storing up God's Word in your heart. Commit today to memorizing a verse or a passage of Scripture that the Holy Spirit can bring to memory when you need it most. If you are new to memorization, start with John 14:5–6. If you're feeling more ambitious, memorize Romans 8:28–39. You can find many techniques online for Scripture memorization. An effective one is the first-letter Scripture memory system. Google it to find out more!

sixteen

He Communicates with Us

I'm thinking about a lovely friend of mine who is newer to faith. She was raised in a home where she was expected to attend church on Christmas and Easter, but she is now beginning to discover the beautiful person of Jesus and His relevance in her everyday life. I have loved watching her friendship with Him unfold. She is astonished by the stories about Him, from the miracles He performed to just the way He lived His life, eating with the outcasts and flipping over tables in the temple. Her journey into Jesus has demonstrated how familiarity with His life can make me lose sight of just how radical He was. I don't ever want to lose the wonder.

This friend also asks the best questions. She is genuinely hungry to know this God of hers more. One question she asked me recently was about communicating with God. She knows people talk about "hearing from God" or "having a conversation with God," but she doubts she'll ever get to "that level," as she said.

Maybe you've wondered something similar. Can you expect God to communicate with you? How do you even know it's God? These are the questions I'm excited to explore now, because the Holy Spirit communicating *to* us and speaking *through* us what

He receives from God is another miraculous benefit to having the Spirit of truth!

He Tells Us What He Hears

Jesus said, "He will not speak on his own; he will speak only what he hears, and he will tell you what is yet to come. He will glorify me because it is from me that he will receive what he will make known to you" (John 16:13–14 NIV).

This means that whatever God wants to say to us is conveyed through His Spirit. And He can be trusted to always say only what He hears from God.

Have you ever played the silly game of telephone, where a group of people sit in a circle and one person starts the game by coming up with a long sentence that they whisper into the left ear of the person on their right? Then that person turns to the person on their right and repeats that same sentence into their ear. The ritual continues until every person in the circle has had a chance to pass the sentence on and it makes its way back to the person who began. What inevitably happens is a sentence that started as, "I went to the store to buy a gallon of coffee ice cream, but they were sold out so I bought chocolate chip instead," ends up as, "I went to Disney World to meet Mickey Mouse, but he was sick so I met Donald Duck's sister instead." This is how our communication usually goes, right? Even with our best intentions, we can't always be trusted to pass on exactly what we hear.

> Whatever God wants to say to us is conveyed through His Spirit.

But when God the Spirit passes on what God the Father wants to communicate to us, it is never altered, and it is always and only at God's go-ahead.

124

Not surprisingly, the same is true in the relationship between Jesus and God. The Son never made a move without the leadership of the Father. Jesus himself testified to this when He said,

> Very truly I tell you, the Son can do nothing by himself; he can do only what he sees his Father doing, because whatever the Father does the Son also does.

> John 5:19 NIV

God the Son and God the Spirit are always speaking and working according to the orchestration and leadership of God the Father.

That is wild! God speaks to us. Directly. Personally. Specifically. And the Spirit is the One who makes it possible. May we never take this incredible benefit for granted.

Now let's see how we can expect Him to speak.

The Nudge

In our family we have an expression known as the "Holy Spirit nudge." Nudging is a form of His communication.

Sometimes His nudge guides us to do something or to say something, and sometimes that nudge tells us *not* to do or say that thing. It's the check in our spirit that urges, "Do this" or "Stop that" or "Say this" or "Stay quiet" or "Keep going" or "Wait."

For example, when the boys talk to each other in a way that is not in alignment with who God created them to be, I'll ask, "When you were speaking unkind words to your brother that tore him down, was there something inside you urging you to hold your tongue but you let it loose anyhow?" Or, "When you were not being honest with me about what you did with your friends, did you sense the Spirit nudging you to tell the truth?" If so, that was the Holy Spirit!

I know I feel that nudge all the time.

125

Like the time I saw the homeless woman sitting on the bench outside Dunkin' Donuts as I left the shop with my warm coffee in hand, and the Spirit nudged me to go back inside and get back in the long line to buy her a gift card and tell her God sees her and loves her. So I did. And I'm pretty sure that the surprise in her eyes and the smile on her lips blessed me just as much as the affirmation of being seen by God blessed her.

Or the time I was chatting with a woman sitting next to me at the pool at our neighborhood club and she told me she isn't a "religious person," but her curiosity about Jesus was sparked by something I shared on social media. As she continued to talk, I sensed the Spirit nudging me to tell her how much Jesus loves her, but I was internally fighting with Him while she spoke. *No, no, no. I don't want to freak her out. Please, no. I like having friends.* But the nudge persisted, and I've learned He can be trusted. So I said it. And what happened next blew me away. Tears filled her eyes. "Really? You think so?" she asked. "Oh, girl, I *know* so," I said. And the door was opened for me to share how being a "religious person" is radically different from having a relationship with Jesus.

I also feel His nudge to hold my tongue when I want to unleash it in anger at my child's willful disobedience. Or when I need to swallow my pride and apologize to my husband in an argument. Or when I begin to engage in gossip, or I lack gratitude, or I just have a foul attitude.

But before it sounds like I always respond to His nudge, let me assure you of my humanity. Sometimes I heed the nudge and sometimes I ignore it. And then I either reap the benefits . . . or clean up the mess.

Siri and God's Spirit

A question I know a lot of us ask is, "How do I know if it's actually the Holy Spirit communicating with me or if it's just me convincing myself of something?"

A good starting place for answering that question is by asking these questions: Does what you're hearing or sensing align with the truth of Scripture? Does it align with the character of God? See, the Holy Spirit will never communicate anything that is not in alignment with God's Word, so we always need to test what we sense with what God's Word says. And this is why we need to be in our Bibles! We can't know the voice of God without the Word of God.

Let me tell you a little story about Siri.

I love Siri because I don't like typing my texts or emails. If I read an email on my computer that requires a long reply, I will find my phone to reply just so I can use Siri. I use Siri for almost everything I send.

> We always need to test what we sense with what God's Word says.

When our son Andre joined our family from Haiti at the age of twenty-two, he watched with curiosity as I used Siri to communicate on my phone. After several months of this, he finally said, "Mom, I don't know how you can do that. You just sent such a long text using Siri, and she understood everything you said. I wish I could do that, but she doesn't understand my Haitian accent." We had a good laugh about that, but then I said, "Andre, maybe it's not your accent. Maybe it's just going to take time for her to learn your voice. If you really want to be able to use Siri to dictate your texts, keep talking to her. She'll learn your voice."

Maybe you know where I'm going with this.

An integral part of discerning if what you're hearing is from the Holy Spirit is being familiar with the voice of the Spirit. Just as Jesus said, "My sheep hear my voice, and I know them, and they follow Me" (John 10:27). The voice of the Spirit is Jesus. Jesus gave us the precious gift of the Holy Spirit to speak on His behalf.

But here is what makes Siri and the Holy Spirit radically different: As well as Siri knows my voice, she still gets it wrong—a lot.

Like the time I said, "Siri, text hubby and say, 'Hi, honey,'" but instead Siri sent a message to Mike that said, "Hi, homey." I didn't check it before I sent it, and within seconds Mike's response read, "?????" So I tried again, "Siri, text hubby and say, 'Hi, honey,'" only this time Siri sent something I won't repeat so I don't make you blush, but I'll tell you this: In response my hubby wrote, "I'll get the next train home!" Followed by lots of happy emojis.

Indeed, Siri isn't always trustworthy to pass along the precise message we want to communicate. But the Holy Spirit always communicates with us and intercedes for us in absolute accordance with God's will. This is one of my favorite things about Him. Any time I am at a loss for what to do or what to say, or when I'm confused about whether I should proceed in a situation or wait, I call on the Holy Spirit to tell me what to do. This often happens in those midnight hours when worry tries to grip me as I wrestle with things that feel heavy.

Sister, I may not know what worry is gripping you or what decisions are weighing on you, but may I encourage you to let Him lead you in the decisions before you? He wants to speak into your life and lead you in the plans God has for you!

How He Speaks

Sometimes He speaks through the words of a wise friend, or a lyric of a song, or a verse someone passes along. Our job is to learn His voice so we know it's Him speaking, and this happens by getting into God's Word and spending time with Him in prayer and conversation. Like any friendship, the more time you spend together, the better you know one another. You will learn His voice! It is not for the "next level" Christian, as my friend feared.

Do you long to hear from God? Do you need Him to speak wisdom into the decisions in front of you? Maybe it's what course of treatment to choose for an illness, or what job to take, or which school to send your child to, or where to live. Do you need His nudging to help you keep from sinning, or to help you see opportunities where you can be a blessing? Maybe you need His voice of love to speak into the void in your heart.

He is speaking. Are we listening?

Being led by the Spirit is for any believer who will listen, and what He speaks will *always* glorify Jesus—this is the ultimate assurance that what we hear is the truth spoken by the Spirit. As Jesus said, "He will glorify me" (John 16:14).

And not only does the Spirit communicate *with* us, He communicates *through* us. That priceless gift is ours to uncover in the next chapter.

last but not least

Reflect: How hard or easy is it for you to believe that God speaks to people in this way? About what do you most need to hear from Him today?

Respond: Have you ever felt the Holy Spirit "nudge" you? Consider any time in your life when, upon reflection, you've experienced the Holy Spirit communicating with you in any of the following ways. Circle all that apply:

Do this.

Stop that.

Say this.

Stay quiet.

Keep going.

I am with you.

Wait.

Jesus loves you.

Pray: Holy Spirit, I trust you to communicate with me in complete accordance with God's perfect will for my life. Thank you for this priceless gift of your presence inside me. Help me to discern your voice and give me the courage to follow where you guide. As I seek out the wisdom and guidance of good friends in my life, help me remember I can run to you too. In fact, help me remember I should run to you first. Thank you for always being available and always leading me in truth.

seventeen

He Communicates Through Us

I sat on the side of my son's bed while he was intentionally hidden under the covers. He was grieving a situation in his life that wounded him deeply, and I knew there was nothing I could say that would make things better. So I did what I've heard we're supposed to do: Be present in his pain, offer understanding, but don't resort to pithy sentiments in an attempt to fix it or downplay it.

Is there anything worse than watching your child suffer? I don't think there is, and I think about how gutted God must have been as He watched His Son suffer for us on the cross. Yes, God intimately knows the way our hearts break for our kids.

I would have given anything to have my husband next to me on my son's bed, because he always knows just what to say. He is a communication ninja. I believe this speaks to his tenderness to God's presence and his reliance on God's Spirit. But my husband wasn't home, and looking back, I can see how that was the kindness of God. God wanted me to ask Him to speak through me. This moment wasn't on *me*, it was on God.

While we sat in silence, I prayed. I didn't pray aloud, I just whispered in my heart to the Holy Spirit. I prayed for my son to know God's comfort in his sadness and God's hope in his hopelessness. I asked my son's heavenly Father what He wanted His son to know. I asked Him to supernaturally speak through me because I knew this was a crucial moment in my son's life and I didn't know what he needed to hear. I had advice and good ideas, but my son needed more than I had to offer. He needed the Spirit's comfort and wisdom.

And here's what I want you to know: I didn't have complete faith that God would give me what I needed to say. As I silently prayed, begging God to help me speak His words of hope over my son, I wondered if it would "work." But I thought, *What do I have to lose?* As you can see, I'm filled with faith, until I'm not.

Several minutes later, when my son lowered the covers and invited conversation, the words God gave me were so unlike the mama-bear words I would usually use. So much so that I think I even surprised my son. God gave me what my son needed to know.

> He takes the thoughts of God and the things of God and He makes them known to us and through us.

When I told the story to my husband later that night, his smile stretched wide when he said, "That's beautiful, babe. Tell me what God said!" But I couldn't. Not really, at least. I could barely remember what was spoken to my son by the Spirit of God. But I know it planted hope, and I know it provided Spirit-filled wisdom. I know it settled in his soul because I could see it in his eyes. The Holy Spirit worked supernaturally in our hearts. He spoke through me, not because of anything I bring to the table or because of my great faith (as was demonstrated by my doubt), but because He lives in me and it's what He delights to do. He spoke through me because I made myself available to Him. He takes the thoughts of God and the things of God and He makes them known to us and through us.

He Is an Excellent Communicator

We see a pattern of the Spirit speaking not just *to* people but also *through* people throughout Scripture, so we shouldn't be surprised that this is something He still does for us today. He speaks through us now if we offer ourselves as vessels.

The Holy Spirit is a skilled communicator. He knows what to say when we are at a loss for words or need to speak into a difficult situation. He knows what to pray when we don't know what we need or want. He can help us articulate the feelings we can't make sense of or are too afraid to say. He can help us speak in precarious situations.

For example, when Jesus was speaking to His disciples about being on guard when they are accused on account of Him and face severe persecution, He assured them, "Do not be anxious beforehand what you are to say, but say whatever is given you in that hour, for it is not you who speak, but the Holy Spirit" (Mark 13:11).

The assurance for us is that if the Holy Spirit can help the disciples speak in such dire circumstances, how much more can we count on Him to speak to us, and through us, in our daily struggles and darkest battles. Hear Jesus saying to you even now, "Don't be anxious, daughter, because my Spirit will teach you what to say."

"For it is not you who speak, but the Holy Spirit" is something I often encounter when I'm writing. I ask the Holy Spirit to speak *to* me when I study the Word of God, and *through* me when I put my fingers on the keyboard. Then I count on Him to show up as He says He will.

I used to feel arrogant saying that, like, *Who am I to suggest that God gives me what to say when I write about Him?* It felt bold to suggest that my writing was guided by God. But that nonsense was replaced with the truth that this is a gift given to *every* believer. It doesn't make me special. It makes me His. God's Spirit inspires every human soul who puts their hope in Jesus—all for His glory.

John Piper writes, "The words of Jesus have already been given to us. The four Gospels, formed out of Jesus's teachings, are a mountain of treasures. We are to listen to the words of Christ (Mark 9:7), give them a home in our minds (John 8:37), and treasure them (Colossians 3:16). This is the raw material that the Holy Spirit works with as he teaches us what to say. He inspired the words of Jesus the first time. He loves to use them when the time comes."[1]

Dance with Me

I also experience the Spirit's inspiration when I speak, but there is one occasion in particular that I deeply cherish. A few years ago, I was the speaker at our church's annual women's retreat. On the evening of the opening session, the women on the worship team gathered and asked to pray over me. Never had I been so grateful for the ministry of prayer. I think they could see the burden I was carrying. I was feeling the pressure to "perform" well on stage even though the genuine cry of my heart was to lift my King Jesus high.

As the women prayed aloud, I felt the heaviness lift. The very thing I was speaking about over the weekend—"It is for freedom that Christ has set us free"[2]—became immensely real to me in our prayer time. The Holy Spirit was settling on me, stripping away the pressure to impress the crowd, and stirring in me a sense of assurance that God—and God alone—was going to do something extraordinary *through* me. An undeniable sense of His presence (calmness and confidence) came *upon* me and I knew He would work *through* me.

The last person to pray in the circle was our pastor's wife, Anne. Anne has the most tender heart for God, and the way she leads worship is a testament to that. I don't remember every word of her prayer, but this is a short summary of what she spoke over me: "Jeannie, I have this picture of you in a dance with Jesus on the stage, the Holy Spirit orchestrating your steps as you follow the

Lord's lead. Jesus wants to dance with you as you allow the Spirit to speak through you." Well, there went *all* my makeup. I wiped the tears from my cheeks and the snot from my nose and walked to my seat for the worship time that preceded my talk.

But I think it actually did all of us a world of good to have me take the stage with puffy red eyes and a heart that had just been melted by the Lord's love. I knew He had empowered me for the call.

"Dance with me" was the invitation I heard over and over again throughout the weekend. I was so captivated by the ever-present sense of His Spirit. He spoke through me to bless His bride, the church, that weekend.

This is precisely what Paul was talking about when he said, "My message and my preaching were not with wise and persuasive words, but with a demonstration of the Spirit's power, so that

> God wants us to speak with Spirit-taught words.

your faith might not rest on human wisdom, but on God's power. . . . This is what we speak, not in words taught us by human wisdom but in words taught by the Spirit, explaining spiritual realities with Spirit-taught words" (1 Corinthians 2:4–5, 13 NIV).

Just like Paul, we are encouraged to let our words be a demonstration of the Spirit's power. God wants us to speak with Spirit-taught words. This is an incredible benefit to having the Holy Spirit.

Friend, King Jesus wants to dance with you. Can you let that just settle on you? As you dance, the Holy Spirit will orchestrate your steps and guide your speech. So whether you are stepping up to a microphone, shepherding hearts at home, speaking with difficult colleagues, sharing coffee with a friend, or struggling to articulate your needs to your spouse, you can ask—and count on—the Spirit of God to communicate through you and give you words that will glorify God.

last but not least

Reflect: Which of the following scenarios have you experienced?
- I didn't know what to say in a difficult situation.
- I was at a loss for words when I wanted to comfort a friend.
- I felt uneasy praying out loud.

Read 1 Corinthians 2:1–5, 13. How do Paul's words bring assurance to you now?

Respond: Sometime today, ask the Holy Spirit for specific direction on how to communicate. Don't be surprised if you sense that your words are, as Paul wrote, "very plain." Perhaps as plain as "I'm so sorry," "I am here," "Can I pray for you?" "I love you." Then respond by speaking those words over someone who needs to hear them.

eighteen

He Makes God's Love Real to Us

One of the ways I experience the Holy Spirit's presence is through the affection I feel toward Jesus. The Holy Spirit makes me want to worship Jesus by stirring up immense gratitude in my heart that often leads to tears welling up in my eyes. It's no wonder my boys often ask, "Mom, why do you get so teary when you sing about Jesus?"

For example, one typical morning before school, I opened our family devotion and read the day's passage. The reading that morning was about the crucifixion, and I couldn't get through it without feeling the weight of it. The thorns on His brow. The nails in His hands. The abandonment of His Father. The sin of the world. Every single sin of mine. On Him. I bit my lip and let tears collect in my eyes. I held my breath and let the enormity of God's sacrifice convict me and comfort me. It was only seconds, however, before one of my boys exclaimed, "She's crying again!"

"These are grateful tears, boys," I replied. "I'm just so amazed by Jesus and grateful for what He has done for us. The tears are my response to the Holy Spirit making His love real to me. That's what the Holy Spirit does. He makes us tender to the love of God."

I also assured them that my tenderness to Jesus isn't proof of my godliness. It's actually proof that I'm aware of my ungodliness. I know how much I need grace. I know who I've been rescued by and I know what I've been rescued from, and my soul can't *not* respond.

I believe I'm starting to sound a bit dramatic, so I want to be careful with my words because drama is not characteristic of the Holy Spirit. He doesn't attract attention to himself. Extreme emotionalism isn't part of His personhood. But what He *does* do is attune our hearts to the love of Jesus. And the love of Jesus *should* move us. It's beautiful beyond description.

Have there been moments in your life when you've just wanted to marinate in the Lord's love? When you just wanted to stand and worship Him with abandon? When you've just wanted to sit in the silence of His tender presence? That is the Holy Spirit at work! He shows us there's nothing better than God's love. But let it be said, someone's tenderness to Jesus can be quiet and internal, and another person's can be vibrant and external. But one thing is for sure: If it's the Holy Spirit, it won't be unnoticeable. My one encouragement would be not to fear opening yourself up to how the Spirit wants to stir in you an affection for and tenderness to Christ.

Like a groom waiting at the altar, eager to lift the veil to see the beauty of his bride, the Holy Spirit is eager to lift the veil and reveal the beauty of God in Jesus Christ to us.

Intimacy with God

On summer evenings, we love to have friends over for dinner in the backyard. While the kids roast marshmallows and play basketball, we linger under the string lights at the outdoor table long after the meal is over. It's actually as idyllic as it sounds, at least until someone gets stabbed with a marshmallow stick.

One evening, our conversation turned to the Holy Spirit, and in particular, intimacy through the Holy Spirit. Our friend, who is a pastor, said that intimacy with Jesus is one of his favorite things to teach because, as he said, "Who doesn't long for intimacy? We all do!" He came more and more alive as he spoke about what he has witnessed happen in people who have had the revelation that they can feel closely connected to God through His Spirit. "Awakening to the intimacy of the Holy Spirit completely changes people," he said with enthusiasm.

Paul taught about how the Holy Spirit helps us experience the love of God when he wrote, "God's love has been poured into our hearts through the Holy Spirit who He has given to us" (Romans 5:5).

Paul isn't likening the love God gives us to the slow drip of a leaky faucet. It's more like Niagara Falls. God is profusely *pouring* His love into our hearts because He longs for loving and intimate relationship with His children. We worship a God who is both omnipotent *and* intimate!

Of all the things the enemy does not want you to experience, I believe intimacy with God is at the top of the list. He knows he's done once you discover there is no substitute for it and no greater joy found outside of it. To feel truly known by God and to experience the warmth of His presence and His welcoming acceptance is better than the best this world can offer, and the enemy knows that.

> We worship a God who is both omnipotent *and* intimate!

That being said, I realize that the idea of intimacy with God can make some feel uncomfortable, especially if they were raised in a home where God was seen as a distant being rather than a relational Father. But deep familiarity and rich fellowship with God is one of the most treasured gifts the Holy Spirit gives us, so if intimacy feels foreign or uncomfortable to you, would you dare to ask the Spirit to pry your heart open to the great flood of love He wants to pour in? The Holy Spirit beckons you to call the "Alpha and Omega" your "Abba, Father."

God as Abba Father

Knowing how much God longs for intimacy with His children, it shouldn't surprise us that *Abba* is the Aramaic word Jesus used for *Father* in the Lord's Prayer. This is an informal name we would often translate in the English language as *Daddy*. Think about that for a moment. We are invited into sacred intimacy with the Trinity.

> The Holy Spirit beckons you to call the "Alpha and Omega" your "Abba, Father."

Paul writes about our intimacy with God this way: "You have received the Spirit of adoption as sons, by whom we cry, 'Abba! Father!' The Spirit himself bears witness with our spirit that we are children of God" (Romans 8:15–16).

Do we see what's happening? The Spirit enlivens a sense of belonging in our hearts. Belonging! While the enemy is tapping into our insecurities that tell us we are unwelcome and unwanted imposters in God's presence, the Holy Spirit is melting our hearts with the assurance of our adoption as God's precious one.

Why does this matter? Because an intimate relationship with God is central to the flourishing Christian life, and the difference in those who experience intimacy with God and those who don't is typically rooted in our openness to the Spirit and our obedience to God's Word.

God has personally poured His Spirit into our hearts so we can have a deeply personal and life-giving relationship with Him. Let's not miss it, friends! Let's not settle for rote religion when we can have real relationship with our Abba Father!

last but not least

Reflect: Read Galatians 4:6–7. Reflect on the truth that you are an heir of God, and you inherit all the blessings and benefits as a daughter of the King.

Respond: Ask the Holy Spirit to stir up gratitude and worship in your spirit for all of the ways you are a beneficiary of God's grace. Salvation, healing, wholeness, intimacy, peace, belonging, favor, and intimacy with God are yours because of Jesus!

nineteen

He Convicts Us

I have a friend who isn't afraid to call me out when she sees things in my life that aren't in alignment with God's best for me. Maybe it's about an unhelpful attitude I have about something, a questionable decision I'm making, things I'm prioritizing, or a false narrative from the enemy that I'm believing.

I deeply value this aspect of our friendship, as I actually *count on her* to call me out because I know her purpose is always to help me live a life that points to Jesus. I realize that "calling someone out" can at times have a negative connotation and it can leave the person feeling exposed and vulnerable, but this is never how my friend makes me feel. I know whatever she says is *always* said out of love and for my good.

Do we know this is also something our Friend, the Holy Spirit, does for us? He calls us out. Said differently, in theological language, He convicts us. He lovingly convicted me in the counseling session with my husband when I was holding on to bitterness and He continues to convict me on the daily of sin that needs to be dealt with.

I think this could be one of the things we take most for granted about Him. He's the Friend who will faithfully call us out because of how much He loves us and wants to mold us into the likeness of Jesus, for the glory of God. Conviction is His gift of love.

But for many, conviction isn't seen as a work of the Spirit's love. It feels more like an accusatory word. I have a friend who physically shudders when she hears the word *conviction*, because it was used as a weapon against her when she was young. "The conviction of God" felt more like a death sentence than a freedom song.

> Conviction is His gift of love.

Conviction is how the Holy Spirit convinces us or persuades us about what is right and holy. Conviction is not condemnation. When we sin and fall short of the glory of God, we need to know the vast difference between the voice of condemnation and the voice of conviction.

Conviction comes from the Holy Spirit. He beckons us to run to Jesus, repent, receive mercy, and run the race before us in His transforming power and grace (Romans 3:23–24). The purpose of conviction is reconciliation.

Condemnation comes from the enemy. The devil's purpose is to ensure we believe that our heavenly Father is shaking His head at us in disappointment and disgust, with His arms crossed and His heart closed. Condemnation is shaming and it results in us running *from* Jesus in fear rather than *to* Him for forgiveness.

In the next chapter, we will study our astounding freedom from condemnation and shame in Jesus, but for now, let's explore the benefits of the Spirit's convicting work.

How His Conviction Works

Jesus taught that the Holy Spirit would convict us concerning three things: sin, righteousness, and judgment. He explained,

"Concerning sin, because they do not believe in me; concerning righteousness, because I go to the Father, and you will see me no longer; concerning judgment, because the ruler of this world is judged" (John 16:8–11).

So let's look at each of these three things to discover just how significant His convicting work is!

He Shows Us Our Sin

First, how does the Holy Spirit convict us "concerning sin"?

The word *convict* can be likened to the word *convince*. The Spirit convinces us we need Jesus because of our sin. Without this work of the Holy Spirit, we would stay spiritually dead in our sin and not receive new life in Christ.

And His conviction continues after we put our trust in Jesus. The Holy Spirit's job is to go on illuminating our sinfulness, convincing us of its harmfulness, and persuading us to choose obedience. His conviction is intended to protect us from the pain and harm that sin inflicts on our lives and on the lives around us, and to show us the ways in which it separates us from God's best for us. His purpose is to turn us away from sin and to make us more like Jesus.

He Shows Us Our Security

Second, Jesus says the Holy Spirit convicts us concerning righteousness. This means that the Holy Spirit shows us our security in our Savior. That sense of peace we experience about our salvation is the work of the Holy Spirit.

Do you ever fear that God might turn His back on you, or worse, abandon you, because you keep stumbling into that same sin? The Holy Spirit wants to free you from that baseless fear! He wants you to rest in the security of Jesus' sacrifice.

Watch how this goes down.

So first, the Holy Spirit convicts us of our sin, showing us how impossible it is to meet God's high moral standard, which is not only perfection in our outward actions but also perfection in our heart life. God's law requires *more* than good external behavior. His high standard is a pure and perfect *heart*. A heart that loves Him above *all* else. Meaning, doing the right thing with the wrong motive still fails to meet the moral standard called for in Jesus' Sermon on the Mount. So even if we think we are getting it all right in our outward actions, we aren't getting it all right in our hearts—at least not to the extent that God's law demands. But once again, what seems like bad news is actually the doorway to the Good News!

He wants you to rest in the security of Jesus' sacrifice.

Then, the Holy Spirit shows us how the complete righteousness that God requires was satisfied by Jesus. Jesus was not only pure and perfect in His outward behavior. He was pure and perfect in His heart, on our behalf. And because of Him—and only because of Him—we are declared righteous before God! This means we are made right with God because we are covered in the perfection of His Son.

The Holy Spirit reveals our brokenness *so that* we will *finally be set free* from trying to achieve an unachievable righteousness. He reveals our desperation *so that* we will *fall in awe and wonder* at the feet of the One who achieved righteousness for us.

He Shows Us Jesus Won the Victory

Lastly, the Holy Spirit convicts us concerning judgment. This means, quite simply, that the Holy Spirit convinces us that Satan, the former ruler of this world (John 12:31 and 14:30), was defeated when Jesus defeated death. The Holy Spirit convinces us that the enemy no longer holds authority over us. He has been judged by Jesus and he lost.

When Satan tempts you to believe that your sinful nature still holds authority over you, remind him whose power resides inside you. The Spirit of Almighty God! Through the indwelling Holy Spirit, you have the supernatural power to defeat the enemy's temptation. Victory is yours in Jesus' name.

The Holy Spirit makes us aware of our sinful nature to lead us to acceptance of our sinless Savior. Then He empowers us with the confidence that we hold the victory over slavery to our sinful nature. What an extraordinary benefit His conviction is!

last but not least

Reflect: Read Ephesians 2:1–10. Identify a time when you sensed the Spirit's conviction.

Respond: Thank the Holy Spirit for "convincing" you of your need for Jesus. Thank Jesus for His perfect righteousness that has you completely and unequivocally covered. Ask the Spirit to empower you to walk in victory over those sins that still battle for your affection, and choose one specific way you can be intentional today in defeating the enemy's temptation.

twenty

He Helps Us Live in Freedom

On June 19, 1865, approximately two months after Confederate General Robert E. Lee surrendered, Union General Gordon Granger traveled to Galveston, Texas, to tell the enslaved African Americans that the Civil War had ended and to inform them of their freedom.

This announcement finally put into practice the Emancipation Proclamation for the slaves, which had been issued more than two and a half years earlier by President Abraham Lincoln.

It's unconscionable to think that for more than two and a half years, people who were set free were still living enslaved simply because nobody told them they were free. And yet, before June 19, 2020, most white Americans had little or no knowledge of this historic day. I certainly didn't. But now we know. And now we will celebrate with great jubilation Juneteenth, the day that people who were already free began to actually live free. Yes, we have a very long way to go, but we're not where we were!

When there was a great deal of conversation about Juneteenth in the news, I thought about how many Christians are doing something similar in their walk with Jesus. We've been set free but we're not living free. Jesus removed the shackles of sin and death, but so many still live under a shroud of shame, and it's often because nobody has told them the extraordinary news of the Holy Spirit's power to help them live free.

I love how Paul opens Romans 8—a chapter that mentions the Holy Spirit twenty-two times—with such unwavering certainty. He declares, "There is therefore now no condemnation for those who are in Christ Jesus. For the law of the Spirit of life has set you free in Christ Jesus from the law of sin and death" (8:1–2).

Paul didn't say "there is now only a little condemnation"— which is just enough to keep you afraid of sinning again. He said there is now *no* condemnation. None. Jesus absorbed both our sin *and* shame on the cross. We don't have to wallow in shame when we stumble in sin.

Oh, how I wish that truth had sunk into my heart earlier in my life. See, I always knew that Christ's finished work on the cross covered my sin, but I never heard the good news that He also took my shame upon himself. I thought shame was the thing I was supposed to carry as my consequence for disobedience. I was living forgiven but not free.

> Grace, not shame, is what makes us want to change.

But when the Spirit opened my eyes to the radical grace that not only covers my sin but also lifts my shame, I finally began to experience the freedom for which Christ has set us free. I discovered not only the saving power of grace but also the freeing and transforming power of grace. I discovered that grace, not shame, is what makes us want to change—to turn from sin and run toward life in Christ.

The "Spirit of life" Paul speaks of in Romans 8:2 is the Spirit of the living God. This is yet another example of why we need Jesus *and* the Holy Spirit. The Spirit of life carries out the freedom that was bought by Christ! It's like the freedom baton was passed from the Son to the Spirit. Jesus bought it. The Spirit applies it.

Indeed, "Where the Spirit of the Lord is, there is freedom" (2 Co-rinthians 3:17). Real, game-changing freedom. We are free to take a long, deep breath, let the burdens roll off our backs, and exhale relief. Life and peace are ours to enjoy.

We Are Spirit-People

When Paul writes about freedom, he never means that we are free to do as we please. He means we are free to do what pleases God. We are free *from* the unbearable burden of perfect obedi-ence as the means for gaining God's favor, and we are free *to* live in accordance with our identity as children of God through the life-giving Spirit—and to know the freedom from sin and shame that it brings!

Paul then continues in chapter 8 to say, "For those who live according to the flesh set their minds on the things of the flesh, but those who live according to the Spirit set their minds on the things of the Spirit. For to set the mind on the flesh is death, but to set the mind on the Spirit is life and peace" (Romans 8:5–6).

This passage is not about the believer's struggle with sin! Its purpose is to show us how "according to the flesh" and "according to the Spirit" are two mutually exclusive ways of life. Its purpose is to show us very plainly what we are given as "Spirit people"—life and peace.

This is what we need to know: We are either controlled by the flesh or we are controlled by the Spirit. By "controlled by," I mean under the influence of. And by the way, we don't get away with not choosing because we don't want to be "controlled." In fact, by not choosing, we choose to be controlled by our sinful nature. But if we have the Spirit of God living in us, we are controlled by the Spirit (see Romans 8:9 NLT).

Why does this matter? Because as "Spirit people," we have been given the power to enjoy life and peace. These are extraordinary benefits to having the Spirit. But we have to be setting our minds on the things of the Spirit to reap the benefits. It's an intentional pursuit.

What Will We Choose?

Jennie Allen writes, "The greatest spiritual battle of our generation is being fought between our ears. What we believe and what we think about matters, and the enemy knows it. And he is determined to get in your head to distract you from doing good and to sink so deep that you feel helpless, overwhelmed, shut down, and incapable of rising to make a difference for the kingdom of God."[1]

Jennie then poses the question, "So what is the one thought that can successfully interrupt every negative thought pattern? It's this: *I have a choice*. That's it. The singular, interrupting thought is this one: *I have a choice*. If you have trusted in Jesus as your Savior, you have the power of God in you to choose!"[2]

> We have the power to choose what we set our minds on!

We have the power to choose what we set our minds on! We have the power to take contaminated and condemning thoughts captive to what God says is true about us. This power comes through the life-giving Spirit. And yes, it is absolutely possible for you and for me to take hold of it.

May I ask what condemning thoughts are taking up space in your mind and playing on repeat?

Are you less valuable than other women? Is your purpose insignificant? Are you a bad mom? Are you unlovable? Are you unwanted? Have you made too many mistakes to be of any use to building God's kingdom? Are your addictions eliminating you from being worthy of God's grace? Are you not creative enough, courageous enough, smart enough, or skinny enough? Are you unable to live victorious over a sinful pattern?

Here is the truth! You have the supernatural power of the Holy Spirit to choose what to do with each one of those condemning thoughts. This is the power *of* God *in* you.

Choosing Truth

For too many years, the lie that relentlessly bombarded my mind was that God was disappointed in me. I believed my inability to be a sinless Christian meant I was letting Him down. I was living "under the law" and it was crushing. I felt like a failure in my Father's eyes. That was the negative thought pattern that continually kept me striving to be perfect so I could earn back God's love—a love that, unbeknownst to me, was still entirely mine because of the perfect righteousness of Christ covering me.

See, sometimes condemnation shuts us down and keeps us from pursuing the good works God planned for us long ago. And sometimes condemnation sends us into overdrive, seeking to prove we can still be worthy of God's welcome and of some value to the kingdom. And neither leads to life and peace.

It wasn't until the Holy Spirit enlightened the eyes of my heart to Romans 8 that I began to live freely. I began to hold every lie up to what the Word of God says. I had to set my mind on truth. This is the way of life and peace—rehearsing God's life-giving truth to reject the enemy's life-stealing lies. Do the work. But—and this is an important *but*—remember that the Spirit inside you applies the truth. So while you do the work, ask the Holy Spirit to make it penetrate your spirit. He is the One who applies the truth you feed your mind.

I should also mention we are fighting a battle that has already been won! Do you know this? The power of the Spirit at work inside you is greater than the pull of sin and lies at work against you.

We aren't waiting for the results to come in. Those who belong to God and have the Holy Spirit already have the victory (see 1 John 4:4).

Friend, Jesus set you free. Now the Spirit is in you to help you live free. You've received the good news. Now go and live like it's true, because it is!

last but not least

Reflect: In 2 Corinthians 3:17, Paul writes, "Now the Lord is the Spirit, and where the Spirit of the Lord is, there is freedom." Reflect on what this benefit means for the places you feel stuck or enslaved and lack "life and peace."

Respond: Invite the Holy Spirit to infuse His freedom-filling presence into places where you still live enslaved and stuck. Write a prayer of thanks below, or in your journal, for the freedom the Spirit applies in your life.

twenty-one

He Empowers Us to Obey

It was a quiet morning at the beach. I'd gone out just after sunrise with my son Finn to play in the sand before the tide came in. Only a few other families were there, and all was calm. Until, that is, I heard another mom, just a few feet behind us, trying to convince her toddler to stop walking away from her while she kept an eye on her baby. She kept calling for him to return, but he kept moving away. Finally, out of desperation she yelled, "If you don't come back here, I'm not taking you to Disney World next week!" He wasn't swayed, so she went with a bigger threat. "If you don't come back here right now, you will never, in your whole life, go to Disney World. I'm serious, Danny. Never!" He stopped briefly, I'm assuming to consider what was at stake, but then he continued meandering farther down the beach. She finally had to scoop up the baby and chase her toddler down.

I'm not sure if that little boy ever made it to Disney World, but I do know he wasn't motivated by his mom's threats. Oh, I'm not judging. I've been there. I've threatened some pretty ridiculous things in desperation to get my kids to obey. Always a bad idea!

153

It's easy to fall into the laziness of trying to get my children to obey by ensuring they know the rules and then motivating them by putting into effect consequences that will deter them from breaking the rules. But we see something very different when it comes to the way the Holy Spirit helps us obey.

The Holy Spirit motivates us by making Jesus beautiful to us. The Holy Spirit makes Jesus beautiful to us by awakening our hearts to all that Jesus accomplished for us. He knows that obedience will feel burdensome until Jesus is beautiful. But in light of what Jesus accomplished for us, obedience stems from desire more than duty. But He doesn't stop there. He also provides the power to help us fight our weaknesses and win, because He knows that even our best intentions to obey will fall short without His help.

> Obedience will feel burdensome until Jesus is beautiful.

This is what happened to the disciples the night before Jesus was to be betrayed.

Jesus went with His disciples to the garden of Gethsemane and He said to them, "'Stay here while I go over there and pray.' Taking along Peter and the two sons of Zebedee, he plunged into an agonizing sorrow. Then he said, 'This sorrow is crushing my life out. Stay here and keep vigil with me.' Going a little ahead, he fell on his face, praying, 'My Father, if there is any way, get me out of this. But please, not what I want. You, what do *you* want?'" (Matthew 26:36–39 MESSAGE).

Jesus asked His disciples to keep watch while He left to pray, but when He returned to His disciples, He found them sleeping. He went away two more times to pray, and both times He returned to see them slumbering.

But here's what gets me every time. When Jesus woke them, He didn't condemn them or scold them. Instead, Jesus stated what we know to be true of ourselves: "The spirit is indeed willing, but the flesh is weak" (Matthew 26:41).

In this passage, Jesus is speaking of the human spirit, not the Holy Spirit. The word for "spirit" here is the Greek word *pneuma*, which refers to the soul and mind of man. The word "flesh" here refers to our human nature in all of its frailty. So while our human spirit may try to muster up what it takes, our human flesh fails.

What Jesus said next should undo us.

He said, "Sleep and take your rest later on. See, the hour is at hand, and the Son of Man is betrayed into the hands of sinners. Rise, let us be going; see, my betrayer is at hand" (Matthew 26:45–46). Though they failed Him again and again, Jesus forgave them and welcomed them to remain with Him all the way to the cross. What joy this infuses into those of us who worry that our weaknesses and mess-ups discount us from being valuable to Jesus.

The Spirit Is Willing, but the Flesh Is Weak

Like the disciples, we have our human spirit that is willing, but our human flesh is weak. But unlike the disciples pre-Pentecost, we have the indwelling Holy Spirit. We are not reliant on our human spirit but on the indwelling supernatural presence of the Holy Spirit empowering us!

This is why we need the Spirit's help. The one and only way to obey is letting the Spirit guide us and grant us power. Paul says it so poignantly in Galatians 5:16–17: "Let the Holy Spirit guide your lives. Then you won't be doing what your sinful nature craves. The sinful nature wants to do evil, which is just the opposite of what the Spirit wants. The Spirit gives us desires that are the opposite of what the sinful nature desires. These two forces are constantly fighting each other, so you are not free to carry out your good intentions" (NLT).

Do you feel them battling? Your sinful nature fighting with the Spirit? These two are always at odds. But if we stay motivated by the Spirit—who gives us desires that are pure and pleasing to

God—and we rely on His supernatural power, we are not subject to our selfish ways.

Paul then says, "If we live by the Spirit, let us also keep in step with the Spirit" (Galatians 5:25).

Paul's language to "keep in step" makes it clear we play an active role in the process, because the Holy Spirit will persuade us, but He will never coerce us. As my friend, and theologian, Joel Muddamalle frames it: "Since the Spirit has given us life, we should conform our lives to Him."[1]

Where the Holy Spirit leads, we must follow. Where He guides, we must go. Keeping in step with the Spirit doesn't just happen to us. It requires action.

I have a short story that will bring this home for us.

In Step vs. Side-Step

Our family loves to go on hikes. When you have five boys and a very large golden retriever, the forest is your friend. Our best days are spent on long trails where our boys can jump over big logs, run up steep hills, and splash in shallow creeks.

As we adults know, the trails have cleared paths for a purpose, especially the paths that have steep slopes. I never knew this to be truer than when we explored the extraordinary hiking trails at Yosemite National Park. We told the boys to keep in step with us, so to speak, so they didn't fall into trouble or get lost off the trail. Our instruction wasn't intended to keep them *from* adventure and enjoyment. It was to keep them *in* it. It was for their good.

Similarly, in life, we can keep in step with the Spirit to follow God into the great adventure He has planned for us, or we can side-step Him, wander off and get lost, or fall into the trouble of temptation and sin.

We know what the conversation sounds like when we side-step the Holy Spirit. We say, "I know you are leading me this way, but

I'm stepping over here into deliberate sin." Maybe we even have a longer conversation in which we minimize that sin or justify that sin, but it always means side-stepping the Spirit. It means satisfying the cravings of our sinful nature.

Francis Chan writes, "This does not mean that if you sin, you don't have the Holy Spirit or aren't a follower of Christ. It does mean that when you are sinning, you are not simultaneously submitted to the authority and presence of the Holy Spirit in your life. He is still present, but you are most likely suppressing or ignoring His counsel."[2]

> He will always have our back when we need to fight sin.

What we often forget is that there are consequences to side-stepping the Spirit. And there's a lot more at stake than a cancelled trip to Disney World. Paul warns, "You will always harvest what you plant. . . . So let's not get tired of doing what is good. At just the right time we will reap a harvest of blessing if we don't give up" (Galatians 6:7, 9 NLT).

What stuns me—but it shouldn't because God is so good—is that even when we satisfy the flesh, the Spirit won't cease to exercise His loving conviction in our lives. Our choices may grieve Him and impede Him, but they can't make Him quit. The Holy Spirit is no quitter. He will always have our back when we need to fight sin.

What battle are you presently in? What sin fights for your affection and attention? I have a solid list of my own formulating in my mind even now. I'm guessing you do too! This is because even though our flesh no longer controls us, it still fights to crush us. Though we are no longer enslaved to sin, the enemy still seeks to ensnare us.

But remember, we don't fight alone, friend. We have the authority and the victory in the Spirit to say, "BACK UP, SATAN." Call the devil out. Make it personal, because it *is* personal.

Cooperation with the Spirit

Do you ever wonder why you get stuck in a loop of sin? Do you ask, "Why do I keep doing that again and again?" This is what happens when we aren't letting the Spirit guide our lives. The remedy to this condition is connection to and cooperation with the Spirit!

> We don't have to work up the willpower to stay in step with the Spirit.

Cooperation with the Spirit means yielding to or submitting to His leading in your life. It means learning His voice and choosing His guidance when your rebellious nature wants to go its own way. But even this choice occurs in the power of the Spirit. We don't have to work up the willpower to stay in step with the Spirit. We can't, actually. It comes from God. Paul gives us this great encouragement: "For God is working in you, giving you the desire and the power to do what pleases him" (Philippians 2:13 NLT).

There is a partnership taking place between us and the Spirit. We play an active role, and honestly, it's imperative that we do our part. We have to persevere in Spirit-dependence. Welcoming His supernatural power enables us to be energetic in obedience!

last but not least

Reflect: As you read about how we can side-step the Spirit, did specific areas in your life where you do this come to mind?

Respond: Write below, or in your journal, what makes Jesus beautiful to you. Then take time to pray, asking the Holy Spirit to make Jesus increasingly beautiful to you, so that your heart will be wooed to obey His commands that are for your good and will reap blessing in your life.

twenty-two

He Makes Us More Like Jesus

My friend Meshali Mitchell is a gifted photographer and home-renovator of an 1886 Texas farmhouse. She documents her home restoration journey on her blog, *A House God Is Building*, and I am always so inspired and encouraged by what she posts.

One of the things I love most about Meshali's work, and what makes it so unique, is how she likens the process of her home restoration to the Spirit's sanctification of our hearts. "A House God is Building is my story and it's your story. This home is me; this home is us. A story of what Christ does best by making broken things beautiful and empty things whole," she writes.[1]

While spending an afternoon together, Meshali told me how she can already see what her house can become, but she is doing the work slowly, thoughtfully, with great attention to detail so it reaches its full potential.

The parallels in her home restoration and our heart sanctification struck me. She is patient with the house, like God is patient with our hearts. She isn't cutting corners to get the work done sooner, much like God doesn't cut corners to hurry His sanctification in us. She sees what her house will become, much like

God sees who we will be when He completes His work in us (see Philippians 1:6).

The Process of Sanctification

Sanctification is a glorious benefit for every Christ-follower and a central function of the Spirit in our lives.

To explore the slow process of sanctification, we're going to start in Ephesians 4, where Paul has essentially called out the Gentiles who have surrendered to a sinful life and now insists that those who have put their trust in Christ live as children of God.

Paul writes, "But that is not the way you learned Christ!—assuming that you have heard about Him and were taught in Him, as the truth is in Jesus, to put off your old self, which belongs to your former manner of life and is corrupt through deceitful desires, and to be renewed in the spirit of your minds, and to put on the new self, created after the likeness of God in true righteousness and holiness" (Ephesians 4:20–24).

> We *participate* by our obedience, but we don't *produce* holiness in our lives.

To have "learned Christ" is to know "living in Christ." The process entails putting off our old self—which is taking off those things that previously weighed us down and held us back from living like Christ—and putting on the new self—which is essentially becoming who we *already are* in Christ. By His grace that is at work within us, and with minds set on the Spirit, we are called to live into our *true identity* as children of God.

The English word *sanctification* comes from the Greek word *hagiasmos*, which means to "set apart" for a purpose.[2] We could also say that to sanctify is to make holy. So sanctification is the ongoing process of the Holy Spirit growing us in holiness. We

161

participate by our obedience, but we don't *produce* holiness in our lives—He does! (See 2 Thessalonians 2:13 ESV.)

This is an important distinction, because a lot of us tend to think of sanctification as trying harder to be holier, which only leads to less reliance on the Holy Spirit. But growing in the likeness of Christ can't be accomplished through human grit. It's a work of grace, just like our salvation. Through the Spirit, "you were cleansed; you were made holy; you were made right with God by calling on the name of the Lord Jesus Christ and by the Spirit of our God" (1 Corinthians 6:11 NLT). It's the "by the Spirit of our God" part that we often miss.

The Spirit helps us become more of who God says we *already* are in Christ! And this "becoming" is a lifelong process. I need to be constantly reminded of this because I can get so discouraged and beat myself up good about my sin and my setbacks and my lack of growth. I don't want to keep messing up and falling down and getting back up, but that is how it will look for all of us until we take our last breath. *Then* we will be like Him, when we are with Him. Until then, we are ever growing in godliness.

We were created in the image of God to live in the likeness of Christ. So it makes sense that we feel most alive and most satisfied when we are living into our true identity as children of God in pursuit of holiness.

The Pursuit of Jesus

During a Saturday afternoon walk in our little downtown, I ran into a friend I hadn't seen in quite a while. She and her family live on the other side of town, and our kids are different ages, so we really only see each other at church, but I'd noticed I'd been seeing them less and less on Sunday mornings. This friend and I didn't have much time for catching up, but when I told her I missed seeing her at church and I asked her how they've been doing, she was honest. "I'm not doing great, actually. I'm really frustrated with my faith. I've been trying really hard to be a 'good Christian,' but nothing is changing. *I'm* not changing." If only we *all* had the courage to be that forthcoming. I asked her if we could grab coffee soon, but I didn't leave her without sharing what God is still revealing to me. And that is this: Just pursue Jesus.

The pursuit of Jesus will produce holiness! The closer we get to Jesus, the more we grow in His likeness. We don't change ourselves in that pursuit. The Holy Spirit does. He can't not.

See, nowhere in the Bible are we told to make our aim being *good for Him*. We are told to *behold Him*. Trying to be a good Christian was never God's goal for us. His goal is for us to behold His glory. We are changed by getting to *know* Him better, not in trying to *be* better.

If we want to become more like the One we worship, we need to invest in that relationship. The relationship provides fertile ground for the Spirit to produce glorious fruit!

Indeed, we have a significant role to play in our sanctification. This is why in Hebrews 12:14 the author writes, "Make every effort to live in peace with everyone and to be holy; without holiness no one will see the Lord" (NIV).

We can read this and mistakenly think that Scripture is teaching us to strive for holiness in human strength. That wouldn't be an unreasonable way to read it, outside the knowledge of how God's Spirit works. But if we know that even our "effort" is enabled by the Spirit, we won't get exhausted by this invitation. I once heard a pastor at our church put it something like this: "Put down your paddles and put up your sails. Instead of rowing, take a posture of receiving."

Growth in Holiness

To make every effort to be holy means to be intentionally yielded to the Spirit. Through this yielding, we are invited into the love that dwells among the Three-In-One, and the fruit of the Spirit is manifested in our lives.

163

Oh, and let us know this! Our growth in holiness does not elevate our status before God. We are covered in the complete righteousness of Christ when we first put our trust in Him. Rather, our pursuit of Christ is the proof that the Spirit is at work in our life, purifying our desires and producing holiness in our lives.

And this word—*holiness*—is a beautiful depiction of God's power and goodness. The pursuit of holiness is radical, it is sacrificial, it is even dangerous, in the sense that we take up our cross and follow God's invitation to participate in His work of redeeming creation. There is no greater adventure than saying, "Jesus, I'll follow you anywhere!" Buckle your seat belt after that prayer—life is about to get exciting!

last but not least

Reflect: Read 1 Corinthians 6:11. Fill in the blanks.

"But you were washed, you were sanctified, you were justified in the name of the Lord Jesus Christ and by _____ _____." What do these verses suggest to you about who is doing the heavy lifting of sanctification here?

Respond: Identify some of the ways you have tried to sanctify yourself. Identify a specific way today that you can commit to the pursuit of Christ rather than the pursuit of perfection.

twenty – three

He Produces Fruit in Our Lives

My dear friend Jodie Berndt is writing a book about the practice of abiding. I already know I love it, as all of her previous books on prayer have been a great blessing in my life. My husband and I often say that praying the Scriptures for our children, through the books Jodie's written, is the best parenting tool we have. I am constantly reminded that while I'm busy foolishly trying to fix things in my kids' lives that I have no control over, God is still very much in the business of working miracles through our prayers. Isn't that some good news!

Jodie and I check in with each other often as we write. We share the things God is teaching us through His Word, we cheer each other on, and of course, we pray for each other. What else would you expect from a friend who lives her life steeped in prayer? What a gift she is!

One particular day we were texting back and forth about something we were both writing about—the fruit of the Spirit—and, with her permission, I want to share with you what she texted to me because it's too good to keep to myself. She wrote:

Please tell me you write about the gifts of the Spirit as a plural thing—many gifts for one purpose: the common good. And that you write about the fruit of the Spirit as a singular noun.

I often hear people talk about the fruits (plural) of the Spirit, as though things like patience and kindness and love were to be made manifest in differing measure in our lives. But no. As we grow deeper in relationship with the Holy Spirit, all of His attributes—His fruit—show up in our lives. So what we need to do is just ask for more of the Holy Spirit. And then the love will come . . . along with all of its friends![1]

Jodie is, of course, referring to the well-known passage of Galatians 5:22–23, in which Paul writes, "But the fruit of the Spirit is love, joy, peace, patience, kindness, goodness, faithfulness, gentleness, self-control."

I don't know that I will ever again be able to read these verses without thinking of the *fruit* as *friends* who travel in a pack. But doesn't it just make so much sense when she puts it that way.

Jodie then concluded her text with what I love most: "I feel like you can swap the word 'fruit' for the word 'character.'" Yes! The character of the Spirit is love and all its friends. Love is the Spirit's defining characteristic! He *is* love, He is loving to me, and He manifests love—and all of its friends—in my life. Can we just let that sink in, because this can radically change how we talk with Him and think about Him and enjoy Him. This is a relationship rooted in love!

The Fruitful Vineyard

In John 15:4–5, Jesus says, "Abide in me, and I in you. As the branch cannot bear fruit by itself, unless it abides in the vine, neither can you, unless you abide in me. I am the vine; you are the branches. Whoever abides in me and I in him, he it is that bears much fruit, for apart from me you can do nothing."

Do we see the if/then message in this passage? *If* you abide in me, Jesus says, *then* you will bear much fruit. Said differently, *if* you do *not* abide in me, *then* you can do nothing. I love the imagery Jesus uses here. He "is the one true vine and the fruitful vineyard. By the Spirit's presence in our lives we have entered into an organic union with Him—a union of branches to vine."[2]

> Without the power of Christ working in us and through us, we are incapable of producing fruit that is God-glorifying.

You might read Jesus' words and wish you could ask, "Okay, Jesus, but plenty of people do plenty of things without abiding in you. What do you mean when you say, 'Apart from me you can do nothing'?"

I believe what Jesus is teaching us here is that while we might be productive people without entering into an organic union with Him, we won't be spiritually fruitful people, and there is a profound difference between the two.

Without the power of Christ working in us and through us, we are incapable of producing fruit that is God-glorifying. Even on our best day, filled with good works and good behavior, we know that our actions, and deeper still, our motives, are tainted with sin. We might have the desire to do what is right, but without the power of Christ, we can't execute. As Paul writes in Romans 7:18, "For I know that nothing good dwells in me, that is, in my flesh. For I have the desire to do what is right, but not the ability to carry it out."

Fruit Glorifies the Father

Remember what is going on in the life of Jesus in John 15. We have spent a great deal of time in John 14–16, and we are all aware that in these three chapters, Jesus knows His death is imminent. So it shouldn't be lost on us that the night before He was to be put to death, one of His final exhortations to His disciples was about abiding. Why? So that they might flourish and bear fruit!

Imagine you're a teacher and you've spent three straight years with a small group of students, teaching them everything they need to know for them to thrive and carry on what you've taught them. But now it's time to say good-bye to those students, and you have to highlight what you most want them to remember and hold on to when you depart. You have to take a highlighter to what they most need to know. That's what Jesus is doing. He tells them to abide and then He tells them why.

Jesus says, "By this my Father is glorified, that you bear much fruit and so prove to be my disciples" (John 15:8).

The whole of the Christian life, and the work of the Spirit of God, is to bring glory to God. When we abide in Christ, the fruit is the proof, and the Father is praised. This is what the Holy Spirit does. He wants you to flourish and thrive!

We read something similar in Colossians 1:10 that is worth including, because it relates to beholding and abiding. Paul writes, "Then the way you live will always honor and please the Lord, and your lives will produce every kind of good fruit. All the while, you will grow as you learn to know God better and better" (NLT).

Knowing Him Better

He says we will grow as we come to know God better and better, not as we try harder and harder. We get to know Him better by abiding in Him. As we invest in our relationship with Him and welcome Him into the intimate places of our lives where we've previously denied Him access, our lives will—they can't not—produce every kind of good fruit for the glory of God. Or said differently, when God does not have my attention and affection, the lack of spiritual fruit is the proof.

If this doesn't put to rest the "try harder" mentality of the Christian life, I don't know what does.

Have you tried the "try harder" way? I have. It looks like striving for sinlessness in my own strength. Proving my lovability to God. Performing for His affirmation. It's exhausting. And the fruit of that try-hard way—the fruit of my flesh—looks more like conditional love, circumstantial joy, partial peace, impatience, convenient kindness, self-serving goodness, wavering faithfulness, harshness, and indulgence.

> We will grow as we come to know God better and better, not as we try harder and harder.

But the fruit of the "knowing Him better" way is the fruit of the Spirit. It's the manifestation of the character of God in my life. It's unconditional love, boundless joy, peace outside circumstance. It's patience, kindness, goodness, faithfulness, gentleness, and self-control.

Do these two ways show us the stark contrast between the natural and supernatural?

When we operate in the power of self rather than in the power of the Spirit, our lives will manifest the fruit of self rather than the fruit of the Spirit. Thankfully, the fruit of the Spirit is not a checklist of virtues we are expected to manufacture in our own power. It's the supernatural manifestation of a yielded heart abiding in Jesus. And since fruit is singular, this means we are empowered to bear *all* the fruit when we abide in Him.

Practicing His Presence

So what are the things we can do to abide in and enable supernatural manifestation?

We can make a deliberate effort to begin the day in dependence *on* Him and in relationship *with* Him. Welcome His presence. Ask for His power. Be aware of His provision. Be in continual communication with Him. Seek His illumination as you spend time studying and meditating on God's Word. Invest time sitting in silence before Him to hear His voice. These spiritual disciplines—also known as "practicing His presence"—put us in a posture of receiving from His Spirit, like the life-giving sap of a vine, the nourishment required to produce the fruit. There is absolutely no substitute for it.

The psalmist writes about "the way of the righteous" as one whose "delight is in the law of the LORD, and on his law he meditates day and night. He is like a tree planted by streams of water that yields its fruit in its season, and its leaf does not wither. In all that he does, he prospers" (Psalm 1:2–3).

> "Practicing His presence" puts us in a posture of receiving from His Spirit.

Again, there is a clear if/then here. *If* we delight in God's Word and marinate in its truth, *then* we are like a thriving tree planted by a stream of rushing water that yields healthy fruit. But notice the word *delight*. This tells us something about the heart with which God designed us to do these things.

What does it look like to delight in a friend or a spouse or a child? That is how God designed us to practice the disciplines of abiding—with delight. This doesn't mean we shouldn't pick up our Bibles or go to God in prayer if we aren't feeling delighted by the idea of it. It is often a decision more than a delight. But that decision often turns to delight, as our hearts are softened and melted by His love that meets us in the pages of His Word and in the petitions of our hearts.

last but not least

Reflect: Read John 15:1–8. How have you attempted to produce the fruit of the Spirit the "try harder" way?

Respond: Create space to receive the life-giving sap of the Vine and remind yourself that abiding in Christ is the only way a believer's life will bear the spiritual fruit of perfect love. Consider this: Every day for the next week, identify a specific way you will abide in God for no less than ten minutes and see the difference it makes!

twenty-four

He Fills Us

Some of the most joyful moments of my life have occurred on the campus of Danita's Children's Home in Haiti. Our family travels to Danita's annually, along with some dear friends, and from the moment we step off the bus and into the welcoming arms of the children, we enter an atmosphere saturated with the Holy Spirit. His presence is palpable.

The year we took our first trip there, I had an extraordinary encounter with the Holy Spirit. It was the last night of our trip, and we were invited to join the middle school boys in their dorm room for their nightly devotions. These are beautiful boys who have lost their birth parents through death or abandonment, whose futures are so uncertain and whose lives are not stuffed with material possessions—but they were lifting their voices in unison, worshiping Jesus with their whole hearts, singing, "We fall down, we lay our crowns, at the feet of Jesus. . . . We cry holy, holy, holy, is the Lamb. . . ."[1] Let me just tell you, I was wrecked by the Spirit's presence that fell upon us. I experienced the unimaginable joy and hope of the Holy Spirit that supersedes the most heartbreaking stories.

As we walked back to our rooms at the end of the evening, I said to my friend, "I want to bottle this and bring it home." And that's when it hit me. *This* has already been bottled inside me. I *get* to bring it home. I have access to this kind of joy and this kind of hope because it's the overflow of the presence of the Holy Spirit.

But our "blessings"—as they tend to be called—so easily impede this joy. We fill our lives with lesser things. We try to find hope in what we can make happen and we search for joy in what we can accumulate. But the kids at Danita's don't get to stuff their lives with the cheap replacements we have at our disposal. They fill up on God, and as a result they have an intimacy with Him that most of us miss because we aren't desperate for Him to fill us with His Spirit.

Paul guides us in this way of life when he writes, "Look carefully then how you walk, not as unwise but as wise, making the best use of the time, because the days are evil. Therefore do not be foolish but understand what the will of the Lord is. And do not get drunk with wine, for that is debauchery, but be filled with the Spirit" (Ephesians 5:15–18).

Be Filled with the Spirit

To know the fullness of joy that comes from being filled with the Spirit, we will quickly unpack four things in this passage.

To "be filled with the Spirit" is:

- to be under the influence of the Spirit's presence and power
- a command, not a suggestion
- essential to living the full and abundant life promised to us in Christ
- continual

1. Under the influence

For most of my life, I thought Ephesians 5:18 was mostly about not drinking too much alcohol. I wonder if that's true for you too. It's always been far more about what *not* to do than what *to* do. So while drunkenness is clearly identified in Scripture as sin, we will miss the main point of this passage entirely if our primary focus is on what *not* to do, which is getting drunk, rather than on what *to* do, which is to be filled with the Spirit.

For example, when someone drinks too much, that person is under the influence of alcohol, and their thoughts and decisions are controlled by alcohol. But when someone is filled with the Holy Spirit, that person is under the influence of the Spirit, and their thoughts and decisions are controlled by the Spirit.

Unlike alcohol, which deadens part of the brain and makes us less aware of reality, the Spirit enlightens our minds and awakens us to the reality of what we've been given in Christ. People who are full of the Spirit are "living under the influence" of the Spirit and experience the joy that comes from being full of Him.

2. More than a suggestion

When Paul wrote "be filled with the Spirit" to the Ephesians, it wasn't merely a friendly suggestion to them back then, nor is it just a suggestion to us now. It's not the optional part of our Christian walk and it's not reserved for the next level of your life in Christ. "Be filled" is a command for every Christian. A command for our good!

3. Essential to joyful living

To be filled with the Spirit is to "live a life of joy, sometimes quiet, sometimes towering. Truths about God's glory and Jesus' saving work are not just believed with the mind but create inner music (Ephesians 5:19) and an inner relish in the soul. And because the object of this song is not favorable life circumstances (which can change) but rather the truth and grace of Jesus (which cannot) this heart song does not weaken in times of difficulty."[2]

This explains so much of what we experience when we are at Danita's. They are joyful people because they are filled with the person of the Holy Spirit. To be filled with the Spirit is to be filled with joy!

"Be filled" is a command for every Christian.

I want to be filled with the joy of the Trinity! I'm guessing you do too.

Sadly, many Christians do not enjoy the gifts the Spirit gives, the power He provides, and the limitless benefits He brings into our lives because we are not heeding Paul's command to "be filled."

As Catherine Marshall wrote, "He will come to us and fill us only to the degree that we are willing to be filled. He insists on being a welcome guest in our hearts and beings, never a trespasser or an interloper or squatter."[3]

But I realize the question that might be brewing in your mind at this point is, *But I thought God put His Spirit in me when I put my trust in Jesus, so why is there now a command to "be filled" with what I thought I already had?*

Ah, good question!

Yes, the Holy Spirit is fully present in every believer, but not every believer enjoys the fullness of His presence. Being indwelt with the Spirit at salvation is not the same as being continually filled with the Spirit after conversion.

I appreciate how John Bloom explains it.

The reason we talk about the filling of the Holy Spirit as "an event subsequent to conversion" is because that's how the New Testament usually talks about it. Paul was exhorting born-again Christians when he wrote, "be filled with the Spirit." . . . And almost all of Luke's description of Spirit-fillings occurred to people who were already born again. . . . Just like the same people received repeated fillings of the Spirit in the book of Acts, we also need to be filled repeatedly.[4]

4. Keep at it

To "be filled'" is something we are told to seek continually. The original Greek language used for "be filled" in this verse means a repeated experience. On the daily.

We can go to the Lord with nothing but an empty cup and ask Him to fill it with His Spirit. And He will do it, over and over again.

It's the "continual" part that we will look at next because God's best for us is that we would have a continually Spirit-filled life— one that is under the Spirit's control and caught up in the joy that courses through the Three-In-One.

last but not least

Reflect: The Bible reveals that the Spirit is essential to joyful living. I shared about an experience at the orphanage in Haiti where I felt immersed in the joy of the Lord. Can you think of a time when you have felt deep joy? It doesn't have to be an explicitly religious-sounding event like a mission trip or worship service. It might be something that happened in your own living room, on a walk through the park, or under a beautiful night sky.

Respond: Today, take your empty cup before God and ask Him to fill it with His Spirit. Oftentimes, worship music such as "Overflow" by Red Rocks Worship or "Upper Room" by Hillsong Worship puts me in a posture to receive from Him. Perhaps play a song such as these to immerse yourself in His presence. Close your eyes and focus on the lyrics and fill up on His Spirit.

twenty-five

He Keeps Filling Us

Jesus was tired. He was in the middle of His journey from Judea to Galilee, and the long walk in the blistering heat made Him thirsty. It was around noontime when He came to the Samaritan village of Sychar and "sat wearily" down next to Jacob's well, seeking a drink of water. (See John 4.)

Before we read the rest of this story, I wonder if you're struck by His humanity like I am. Jesus is tired, thirsty, and weary. It reminds me how much He understands everything we encounter and feel. He knows physical exhaustion and bodily stress. Nothing we experience is beyond His comprehension. Sometimes I just have to say aloud to Him, "You understand me," to remind me of the worth of that knowledge.

Soon after He sat down, a Samaritan woman came to draw water, and Jesus said to her, "Please give me a drink."

The woman was shocked at His request because Jews refused to associate with Samaritans. But not Jesus. He doesn't look for the VIP section. And He doesn't ignore those who don't hold sway. Outcasts and rebels are His specialty.

"How is it that you, a Jew, ask for a drink from me, a woman of Samaria?" she questioned (v. 9).

Little did she know how this one question would change her life. See, Jesus knew her story even though she didn't know His. Jesus knew she'd been married five times and was now living with a man she was not married to. Jesus knew she came for water from the well to quench her physical thirst, and Jesus knew He was about to offer her so much more—water to quench her spiritual thirst.

I imagine Jesus' compassion when He answered her, "If you knew the gift of God, and who it is that is saying to you, 'Give me a drink,' you would have asked him, and he would have given you living water" (v. 10).

And I imagine her confusion when she pointed out that He didn't even have a bucket with which to draw water. So again, she questioned Him, "Where do you get that living water?" (v. 11).

Jesus, patient with her questions as He's patient with ours, responded, "Everyone who drinks of this water will be thirsty again, but whoever drinks of the water that I will give him will never be thirsty again. The water that I will give him will become in him a spring of water welling up to eternal life" (vv. 13–14).

A woman whose life is mired in sin and shame, void of the "life and peace" given to us in the Spirit, is being offered the hope of heaven for eternity, but also the joy of salvation in *this* life. Jesus is telling her that if she drinks the water He alone can give, a spring of life will "well up" in her. But . . . she has to drink!

Jesus' response reminds us that no one is off-limits from God's grace and new life in the Spirit.

What Will We Choose?

The woman at the well chose to drink, then a "fresh, bubbling spring" (NLT) welled up in her and the joy overwhelmed her. She left her jug by the well and ran into town to spread the news. His love saved her, and His Spirit propelled her to witness.

Jesus taught something similar about the Holy Spirit when He said, "Whoever believes in me, as the Scripture has said, 'Out of his heart will flow rivers of living water'" (John 7:38).

The fresh "spring of water" in John 4 and the "rivers of living water" in John 7 both speak to the ongoing filling, to overflowing, of the Spirit.

Now comes the all-important question: "How can I live, continually filled, by the Spirit?"

Unfortunately, being filled with the Spirit can't be reduced to following a checklist, and I hesitate to even share the practices below because I never want to suggest we need to check a set of boxes before we can enjoy the Spirit. But it's essential that we know what will make our hearts a welcoming home for the Spirit to well up in.

1. Confess

"If we confess our sins, he is faithful and just and will forgive us our sins and purify us from all unrighteousness" (1 John 1:9 NIV). We don't have to worry that confession will lead to rejection. He will be faithful to forgive!

Ask the Spirit to reveal known sin—the things you did do but shouldn't have done, and the things you should have done but didn't.

Then ask Him to reveal unknown sin, such as areas in your life where you don't even realize you are rebelling. Because "the human heart is the most deceitful of all things" (Jeremiah 17:9 NLT), we need the Holy Spirit to help us get honest about our sinfulness.

> We don't have to worry that confession will lead to rejection.

Finally, ask Him to reveal where there is the sin of self-righteousness, such as the areas where you've convinced yourself you're "good enough" and don't need the grace of God, or where you have been smug about your sin, or where you attempted to satisfy God's holy demand with good works.

A powerful verse that guides me in my own time of confession is this one: "Search me, O God, and know my heart! Try me and know my thoughts! And see if there be any grievous way in me, and lead me in the way everlasting" (Psalm 139:23–24).

2. Repent

The word *repent* comes from the Greek word *metanoia*, which means "to have a change of heart."[1] Repentance is about more than feeling sorry for our sin or regretting the consequences of it. It's a deep sorrow for wrongdoing that leads to an internal change of heart and mind. So go ahead, run into the radical grace of Jesus that changes us.

And if you aren't feeling sorrow for your sin, ask the Spirit to break your heart over the same things that break God's. Ask Him to tenderize your heart to the price Jesus paid on the cross. This isn't about feeling ashamed of yourself over your sin. This is about being freed from the shame of sin. Repentance brings refreshment (Acts 3:19).

> Repentance brings refreshment.

3. Yield

We have to yield our self-centered wills to His if we want to be filled. We have to surrender our lives to the authority of Christ. To help you with this, consider praying this prayer daily: *Everything I am and everything I have is yours. I want you at the center of my life so that everything I desire and do will emanate from you. Help me submit my will to yours.*

4. Abide

Stay attached to the Vine through His life-giving Word, prayer, and a heart of worship.

There is an undeniable connection between being filled with the Spirit and being steeped in the Word. Consider the similarities in Ephesians 5:18–19 and Colossians 3:16.

"Be filled with the Spirit, addressing one another in psalms and hymns and spiritual songs, singing and making melody to the Lord with your heart" (Ephesians 5:18–19, emphasis added).

"Let the word of Christ dwell in you richly, teaching and admonishing one another in all wisdom, singing psalms and hymns and spiritual songs, with thankfulness in your hearts to God" (Colossians 3:16, emphasis added).

"The command to 'Let the word of Christ dwell in you richly' stands in the place of the command, 'Be filled with the Spirit' because the indwelling of the word is the way we experience the indwelling Spirit. If you want to be full of the Spirit, pursue the fullness of the Word," John Piper writes.[2]

5. Ask!

God wants to give us more of himself. He is not a God who withholds Himself from us. Do you remember what we read in Chapter 14 about asking for more of Him? Jesus said, "If you then, who are evil, know how to give good gifts to your children, how much more will the heavenly Father give the Holy Spirit to those who ask him!" (Luke 11:13).

> God wants to give us more of himself.

God will be faithful to give the Holy Spirit to those who want Him.

Also, recognize that filling won't always come with overwhelming feeling. It won't always *feel* like a "fresh, bubbling spring welling up" in us. Yes, oftentimes the filling of joy takes our breath away, and it can happen at the most unexpected times. But don't always count on feeling for the assurance of filling. Count on His faithfulness to do as He said. Ask and keep asking.

6. Repeat

God wants us to keep coming back to Him. He is a daily God. New mercy every morning. Enough manna for each day. Fresh filling.

With these practices in mind, I want to offer this word of encouragement. No matter where you are spiritually at this moment, the filling of God's Spirit is for you! Do you feel like you're failing miserably at the Christian life? The Holy Spirit wants to fill you. Do you still have doubts or fear about who the Holy Spirit is? He wants to fill you. Are you struggling with sin and carrying shame? The Holy Spirit wants to fill you.

> Ask the Spirit to help you want *Him* more than your *sin*.

Bring Him your willingness. Begin there. Be honest with Him. Ask the Spirit to help you want *Him* more than your *sin*. Ask Him to help you trust Him with your life. He loves you and longs to fill you and lead you in enjoying the fullness of His presence.

last but not least

Reflect: How have you tended to think about the "filling of the Holy Spirit"? What beliefs or even misconceptions have you held about what it means to be filled by Him? How is that similar to or different from what you just read?

Respond: Identify which of the six points (can be one or many) you want to grow in to live filled by the Spirit. Consider writing below the specific steps you will take to help keep you accountable. Then thank the Holy Spirit for how He will be faithful to fill you!

twenty-six

He Baptizes Us

I could have just as easily titled this book *How to Lose Friends and Not Make New Ones*. Or here's another one: *How to Kill a Conversation at a Cocktail Party*. These titles would better reflect some of the reactions I get when I answer the question, "What is your new book about?" and I think this is largely because of what we will uncover in this chapter and the next.

See, one of the things that compelled me to write this book was recognizing that most Christians acknowledge the existence of the Holy Spirit but avoid any *experience* of Him, therefore missing out on the enjoyment He offers and the very real power He provides. In many ways, I was one of those Christians.

So I want to begin by acknowledging the complexity of this conversation and reminding us that no matter where we land on the things that can often divide us, *this* we can return to: When we put our trust in Jesus, God puts His Spirit in us. The beautiful and beyond-comprehension person of the Holy Spirit is essential to our faith, as He enables and empowers the life of the believer.

What Is the Baptism of the Holy Spirit?

Because the Bible often uses the same words in different ways, and the same phrases in different ways, we often see words such as *filling*, *baptism*, *blessing*, and *anointing* used interchangeably in the "baptism of the Holy Spirit" conversation.

The chapter you just read on the command to "be continually filled" was about the daily filling we need (but don't always experience) to stay in step with the Spirit.

In this chapter and the next I will focus on "the baptism" as a separate experience that is conscious and decisive and imparts felt power. (Again, these words can be used interchangeably in the right context, but here I am attempting to clarify what makes them unique.)

My hope is that we will glean that there is a profound difference in knowing you have the Holy Spirit versus experiencing His power. And my bold prayer for us is that we will learn to *trust* Him and His activity in our lives. Because isn't that really what it comes down to? Do we trust Him? It's understandable if we're skeptical, considering how His power has been abused and misused. But if we can get a solid biblical understanding of the "baptism *of* the Holy Spirit," I believe we might even grow hungry for His supernatural power in our lives. Here we go!

Baptized "of" and "in" the Spirit

Paul writes, "For in one Spirit we were all baptized into one body— Jews or Greeks, slaves or free—and all were made to drink of one Spirit" (1 Corinthians 12:13).

Paul is speaking about *all* believers when he said "we were all baptized into one body." Meaning, we can rightly say that all Christians have experienced the baptism *of* the Holy Spirit because He is referring to how the Spirit unites us to Jesus and His body, the church.

What Paul is *not* saying in this verse is that all Christians have experienced the "baptism *in* the Holy Spirit"—as described in the Gospels and in the book of Acts. Baptism, as mentioned in the Gospels and in Acts, is a separate experience from being "baptized into one body" at salvation.[1]

> **All Christians have experienced the baptism *of* the Holy Spirit.**

"To superimpose Luke's usage of the baptism *in* the Holy Spirit (in Acts) upon 1 Corinthians 12:13— and to claim that all Christians automatically experience what the earliest church experienced—is incongruous."[2]

Let's look at Acts 1 to see the difference being drawn here. Luke pens these words of Jesus to His disciples:

> And while staying with them he ordered them not to depart from Jerusalem, but to wait for the promise of the Father, which, he said, "you heard from me; for John baptized with water, but you will be baptized with the Holy Spirit not many days from now."
>
> vv. 4–6

In this passage, Jesus is not speaking about the baptism *of* the Holy Spirit that we receive at conversion. The disciples are already born-again believers, so Jesus is not saying they will be converted in the baptism they are to wait for in Jerusalem. It is a different baptism. He is speaking about baptism *in* the Holy Spirit, which is a conscious experience of power, and though it *can* happen at salvation, it is typically a later experience and not limited to the initial moment of regeneration.

To add to that, Luke is not suggesting in this passage that there will be a single-second experience. Rather, we can expect subsequent multiple experiences of God's power throughout our Christian life (whether we call them baptisms in or fillings). For example, "Luke describes the first baptism with the Spirit as being filled—he uses the 'filling' language in Acts 2:4. These are overlapping realities—fullness and baptism."[3]

Clear as mud? I get it. Many hours of sleep were lost during the writing of this chapter. But let's press on!

Extraordinary Power

To summarize so far: At conversion, we receive the baptism *of* the Holy Spirit. It is something we receive with salvation, but it is not typically experienced or felt. After conversion, we can experience baptism *in* (or you could say *with*) the Holy Spirit. This is an experienced power that can happen throughout our life, and the experiences people have will vary greatly.

John Piper describes it as "extraordinary power for Christ-exalting ministry." He says, "The kind of filling and empowering we receive in such experiences are needed again and again and again in the Christian life, and they're not consistently the same. It is right to ask for a 'fresh baptism' or 'fresh filling' or 'fresh outpouring' of the Holy Spirit. My understanding of baptism with the Holy Spirit is that Paul uses a form of this phrase to refer to what happens at the new birth. Luke uses a form of this phrase— quoting Jesus—for the empowering by the Spirit which may or may not include various signs, like tongues or other manifestations."[4]

And, of course, there is water baptism, a decision a believer makes after baptism into Jesus to follow Jesus' example. This is the kind of baptism Jesus was referring to in Matthew 28:19. This is an external symbol of an internal decision. It symbolizes how we were once dead and buried in our sin but are now raised to new life in Christ.

Again, there is a great deal of mystery (and controversy) in this conversation. However, what seems undeniable in Scripture is that Peter's life demonstrates how indispensable the baptism is to witness and walk out God's call. The baptism *in* the Holy Spirit was what filled Him with extraordinary power (Acts 2:4;

4:8; 4:31). And the baptism *in* the Holy Spirit is what fills us with extraordinary power. He was wholly dependent on the power provided by the Spirit to do what He was called to do. We also need this empowering.

He Fills Us for a Purpose

I can think of one such example that happened recently.

I was preparing to start writing this book and feeling terribly incapable of the call. And I don't say that lightly. I was doubting if I heard God clearly, so I called my friend Ami, who knew how much I was struggling, and I told her all my excuses for not pursuing this project. Her response didn't surprise me. "Jeannie, Jesus won't force you to trust Him with this message. He is inviting you to write what He is teaching you, but He will let you choose what to do. But I hope you'll trust Him. We need to read what He wants to show you about His Spirit." I knew she was right, but I was still fearful.

Just a few days later, we attended a service whose speaker was teaching on . . . wait for it . . . the Holy Spirit. Of course, it shouldn't be surprising that a preacher taught on the Holy Spirit, but it is indeed a rare thing for an entire sermon to be centered around the work of the Spirit. And I can only tell you that what I experienced during his talk still feels impossible to explain.

The Holy Spirit felt like a weighted blanket on my body and held me captive to His presence that was permeating the atmosphere. I was barely able to lift my hands to my face to wipe the steady stream of tears falling on my cheeks as the speaker articulated and invited the work of the Spirit in that place.

I left the service stunned and in silence, and all day all I could say to my husband was, "What just happened?" as I tried to process how His presence enveloped me. The Holy Spirit made it impossible for me to do anything other than say yes to writing this book because all I wanted was more of Him. I wanted more of the sweetness and intimacy of His presence. He became so undeniably real to me—all over again—and I had renewed confidence that He would provide the wisdom and supernatural power to write about Him.

Again, everyone's experience is unique, but however you have—or will—experience the baptism, one thing is certain: It provides a profound sense of God's supernatural presence and power.

In Acts 1:8 Jesus says that baptism in the Spirit will bring power to the believer. And just as the disciples were baptized for a purpose (Acts 4:31), so we are baptized for a purpose. And the Spirit's desire is to see us fulfill that God-given purpose. The purpose might be for power over sin, power for a task or calling, or power to share the Gospel.

What Jesus did *not* say is that baptism in the Spirit would always bring the gift of speaking in tongues to the believer. It may accompany the baptism. It may not. Speaking in tongues is a spiritual gift (which we will explore in the next chapter), but it is not proof that the believer has been "baptized in the Spirit." What *is* proof is power. The baptism in the Holy Spirit is experiential and undeniable. When He comes upon you, you know you've been changed, and your life will bear witness to it.

> We are baptized for a purpose. And the Spirit's desire is to see us fulfill that God-given purpose.

But I want to be careful here not to suggest that we should expect the experiential and extraordinary power-producing baptism in the Holy Spirit to be a daily, normative experience. I don't say this to dampen our expectations or to put human limitations on how and when God chooses to manifest himself in His people. I'm simply encouraging us to be cognizant of where the Holy Spirit is continually sustaining us instead of seeking mountaintop experiences or the "high" of the filling. Don't miss out on the million small things He is doing in the microseconds that are forming you. Yes, dare to plead with the Spirit for the baptism in the Holy Spirit. But oh, friend, don't be discouraged if you don't experience it when you expect it. God decides when and how He distributes it. It's our responsibility to desire it.

How Will Our Lives Bear Witness to His Power?

One way our lives will bear witness is through our worship. John writes, "God is Spirit and only by the power of His Spirit can people worship Him as He really is" (John 4:24 GNT). The Spirit produces a heart of praise in His people. What a beautiful picture that is. Because we know the ministry of the Holy Spirit is to magnify and make much of Jesus, it makes sense that the Holy Spirit moves us to bow before King Jesus in humble adoration.

This doesn't mean that we will no longer enjoy or seek human praise. It's in our fallen nature to put ourselves on the throne, but we will also be quick to confess and repent when we do it. We will not habitually seek to steal God's glory. We will not make the ongoing narrative about us. We will only find true satisfaction when we magnify Him.

Another way our lives will bear witness to the baptism is through our desire to obey. I said it earlier but it's worth repeating: Obedience will feel burdensome until Jesus is beautiful. When we are baptized in the Holy Spirit, we are gifted with a renewed power to obey because we have experienced afresh the beauty of Jesus. The sweetness of being in relationship with King Jesus changes our desires. It makes us love what He loves and it makes our hearts break over what breaks His, and that includes our own sin. See, this isn't about being sinless, it's about not living in pursuit of sin. And that is only possible in a heart that has been overwhelmed with the victorious power of the Spirit.

Another way our lives will bear witness is that we will do things we absolutely know we could not have accomplished on our own.

We will know we are functioning in the super-over-natural life. We will talk more about this in the next chapter.

And finally, we will be bold to share the Gospel. We won't be able to contain the joy and withhold the news of the treasure we've found in Jesus.

We witnessed all of this in the disciples after Pentecost—their joyful worship, miraculous works, and bold witness with the goal of glorifying Jesus. And these benefits are entirely ours to enjoy today!

last but not least

Reflect: What beliefs have you held, if any, about baptism *in* the Holy Spirit? How do the words of Jesus in Acts 1:4–8 change or affirm those beliefs? What makes you believe or question whether the baptism the disciples received at Pentecost is still for us to experience today?

Respond: Speak honestly with God about your fears, your hopes, your questions, and your doubts about the baptism *in* the Holy Spirit. Ask the Spirit to guide you in the truth of Scripture about how He still longs to manifest His supernatural power in His people today. Like the wind, the Spirit can't be told when and where to blow, but God does tell us to ask for and anticipate His power. Shall we dare to do that now?

twenty-seven

He Gives Us Spiritual Gifts

In the seventh grade, while attending a private Christian school that was part of a large Presbyterian church, I wrote an essay about the gifts of the Holy Spirit for a class project. Looking back, I realize it would have been wise to ask my parents to read my essay before I submitted it. I was, after all, a Preacher's Kid, whose father led another large Presbyterian church in the area, so I had good reason to ask for their input, but I was at that stage where you think you know all things.

I honestly don't remember much about what I said in that essay, or even why I felt compelled to tackle such a topic at twelve years old, but I do remember it was written under the assumption that I knew far more than I actually did about spiritual gifts. That essay landed me a meeting with my teacher, who was very gracious in helping me see how what I'd written revealed some holes in my understanding of the gifts the Holy Spirit gives.

You probably didn't write an essay on the gifts of the Holy Spirit, but maybe you resonate with having some holes in your understanding. Or perhaps you don't feel confused at all and you just long to learn more. Wherever you land, I am excited to share with you what I've learned since writing my not-so-stellar essay in middle school.

Let's start in 1 Corinthians 12, with the well-known passage on spiritual gifts. I want us to read this together, and then I've taken ten truths we can glean from Paul.

> Now concerning spiritual gifts, brothers, I do not want you to be uninformed. . . . Now there are varieties of gifts, but the same Spirit; and there are varieties of service, but the same Lord; and there are varieties of activities, but it is the same God who empowers them all in everyone. To each is given the manifestation of the Spirit for the common good. For to one is given through the Spirit the utterance of wisdom, and to another the utterance of knowledge according to the same Spirit, to another faith by the same Spirit, to another gifts of healing by the one Spirit, to another the working of miracles, to another prophecy, to another the ability to distinguish between spirits, to another various kinds of tongues, to another the interpretation of tongues. All these are empowered by one and the same Spirit, who apportions to each one individually as he wills.
>
> 1 Corinthians 12:1, 4–11

Okay, let's dive in.

Ten Truths

1. Paul opens his letter about spiritual gifts by stating how much it matters that we have knowledge of them. Paul is stressing that they are not superfluous in the believer's life. This means it's important that you and I understand what the gifts are and which one(s) we possess (v. 1).
2. Paul identifies nine distinct gifts. The gifts are distinct from one another but are meant to function together. In fact, in verses 12–26, Paul makes the correlation between

194

the many parts of the human body—which all work together to make it function and flourish properly—and the spiritual gifts that make the church function and flourish. "The way God designed our bodies is a model for understanding our lives together as a church" (1 Corinthians 12:25 MESSAGE).

3. The nine distinct gifts all come from one Spirit. They are:

   Wisdom

   Knowledge

   Faith

   Healing

   Miracles

   Prophecy

   Discernment of Spirits

   Speaking in tongues

   Interpretation of tongues

   The Holy Spirit empowers them all.

4. Every believer is given a spiritual gift. Some believers may be given more than one gift, but everyone has at least one gift. The Holy Spirit chose your gift(s) specifically for you, and you have a significant role to play in the body of Christ. We need you and the gift(s) God has given you! You may not know your gift(s) yet. That is okay. To help you discern yours, a Spiritual Gifts Survey is provided as an appendix. Twice Paul said we should "eagerly desire the gifts," so there is no better time than now to learn what has been entrusted to you. "To each is given the manifestation of the Spirit" (v. 7).

5. The gifts serve a purpose. They are "for the common good." The gifts are never meant to be for selfish gain or self-glorification. The gifts are always about edification and are meant to bring unification (not division, which

195

sadly, happens often). Knowing that the gifts are meant for the common good is what can change the narrative in our churches from "What am I getting?" to "How can I be serving?" (v. 8).

6. The gifts are to be carried out in love. *LOVE*. In fact, in the very next chapter—1 Corinthians 13—we find Paul's famous letter about love, but what we often miss when quoting parts of this chapter is that Paul is writing about the utmost importance of love in exercising our spiritual gifts. If not exercised in love, our gifts, Paul says, are just annoying noise, worth nothing (1 Corinthians 13:1–3). He is stressing that the *gifts* of the Spirit must be carried out with the *fruit* of the Spirit.

7. Spiritual gifts are, in fact, gifts. I think we tend to overlook the word *gifts* in this conversation. Like our salvation, the gifts are not earned, are freely given, and won't be taken. That's a hard one to grasp. It would make more sense to the human mind if Scripture said God reserves the right to withdraw gifts based on how well we steward them. But that is not so with spiritual gifts. It's no wonder, then, that the New Testament uses the Greek word *charisma* to speak of the spiritual gifts given to believers by the Holy Spirit. *Charisma* means "a gift of grace."[1] Spiritual gifts are gifts of grace, like the unearned and underserved love of God in Jesus Christ. These nine incredible gifts are something God wants us to have and use and enjoy and grow.

8. We don't get to choose our gift(s). No person, no matter how hard they want it or will it, can attain a spiritual gift that the Holy Spirit has not appointed. Gifts are given, not chosen.

9. Spiritual gifts are supernatural gifts. These gifts far exceed our human capability. There is absolutely nothing we can do to manufacture or muster up a spiritual gift in our

lives. All of the gifts reveal God's power and all of the gifts are for God's glory.

10. We are not to envy others' gifts. This makes me think of that expression we use with our kids when they're little and they don't like the meal we've prepared. "You get what you get and you don't get upset." Maybe that sounds harsh. I get it. I have envied the spiritual gifts of certain spiritual giants in my life. But I am humbled when I remember our gifts are to be about the common good, not mere *personal* good or glory.

The Higher Gifts

Paul concludes by writing, "But earnestly desire the higher gifts" (1 Corinthians 12:31). What is this about "higher" gifts?

Higher gifts are those that bring the most benefit to the body of Christ rather than just to a single person. Earnestly desiring the gifts is different from envying another person's gifts. This is about earnestly wanting everything the Spirit has to give you for the common good.

Paul writes something similar in the opening of 1 Corinthians 14 when he writes, "Pursue love, and earnestly desire the spiritual gifts, especially that you may prophesy" (v. 1).

Chapter 14 is primarily about Paul addressing the improper use of speaking in tongues and prophecy in the Corinthian church, and he is teaching about public and private use of the gifts. Throughout this chapter, the gift of tongues is described as the least of the gifts, as seen here in verses 4–5: "The one who speaks in a tongue builds up himself, but the one who prophesies builds up the church. Now I want you all to speak in tongues, but even more to prophesy." Yet somehow, speaking in tongues gets the most attention—and criticism—in our conversations.

Paul repeatedly says he hopes that they will all (don't miss the word *all*) enjoy the gift of tongues because it edifies the person who is praying, but unless there is an interpretation of tongues, it is only for personal benefit rather than the building up of the church. This is why prophecy is considered a greater gift—because it does more than just build up the person with the gift. It is right and good to desire being built up in Christ through speaking in tongues. But let us not neglect the gifts that benefit everyone.

It's also worth noting here that tongues as a prayer language is different from what we read about in chapter 11, where we saw how the disciples at Pentecost were empowered to "speak in other tongues as the Spirit gave them" (Acts 2:4). The gift of tongues we saw at Pentecost is referred to as a missional language. When the words came out of the mouths of the disciples and into the ears of the hearers, the Holy Spirit was the active agent translating the Gospel from the disciple's native tongue into the hearers' native tongue.

> The enemy will do anything to prevent intimacy with Jesus.

Again, tongues is the gift that carries the most stigma because it spooks people who have seen it associated with stranger things. I think the enemy is greatly pleased by this because the gift of tongues is an intimate prayer language, and the enemy will do anything to prevent intimacy with Jesus.

It grieves me that the gifts (some more than others) have been abused, exercised out of pride, and exploited for personal profit, and this has turned many away from the faith. I pray the church can move forward practicing the supernatural gifts *in love*, for the advantage of others, and to the glory of the Father (not self) so we don't miss out on witnessing a mighty work of God in our midst. I believe God wants to show himself and His power to us now as much as ever!

last but not least

Reflect: Read 1 Corinthians 14. (I know it's a big ask, but it will give us a much fuller picture of all the gifts!) What stood out to you most?

Respond:

1. Pray. Ask the Spirit to show you the gifts He's given you and how He would have you use them to help others.

2. Study what God's Word says about the gifts. Let this be only the beginning of discovery and discernment.

3. If you are wondering more about how to identify your gift(s), I recommend that you turn to the appendix at the back of the book to take the Spiritual Gifts Survey.

4. Nurture your gift. Take that next step and be courageous enough to exercise your gift in love. Don't let it lie dormant. God wants to work in you and through you for His glory.

twenty-eight

He Can Be Quenched

When I think about women I know who are impassioned for Jesus, one of the defining characteristics of their faith is their reliance on the Holy Spirit. I have a friend I often describe as a "girl on fire" because not only has she walked through some of the fiercest fires this life can bring, but she burns with love for Jesus and emanates the Holy Spirit's presence.

Holy fire, as we mentioned earlier, is a symbol used throughout Scripture to describe the Holy Spirit. And a life that emanates the supernatural fire of the Spirit is available to every believer. Sadly, too many of us believe we are exempt from emanating His power, but I trust by now we know this to be untrue! Priscilla Shirer writes,

Seeing holy fire in us is what will compel others to get off the fence of indifference and serve Him wholeheartedly. This is the unmistakable element that should differentiate our lives from all others. As the fire of God's Spirit falls afresh on us—gracing us with his favor, empowerment, fruit, and gifts—our lives will be purpose-filled, glorifying to His name and bear eternal fruit. God's Spirit inspires, emboldens, sanctifies, and stirs a holy fervor in the soul of a human, first at the moment of salvation and then ongoingly as the believer is molded into Jesus' image and continually impassioned to fulfill their divine purpose.[1]

The significance of God's holy fire within us is why Paul warns, "Do not quench the Spirit" (1 Thessalonians 5:19 NIV).

One way we quench the Holy Spirit's fire is by not putting to good use the supernatural gifting He has given us or by suppressing the use of His gifts in the church. God has uniquely gifted us, and when we don't use that gifting to fulfill our purpose and edify the church, holy fire will not mark our lives or our gatherings.

Fan into Flame

Because the Holy Spirit has been abused and misused in the church, we have neglected His gifts and, in many ways, even become fearful of His work. But rather than quench the Spirit and treat prophecies with contempt, we are to test the use of gifts against the guidelines of God's Word and keep only what proves true and good for the body of Christ (1 Thessalonians 5:20–22 ref).

But there's more! See, not only should we not put out the fire, we should actively seek to keep it burning—blazing, in fact! This is what Paul writes about in his letter to Timothy: "For this reason I remind you to fan into flame the gift of God, which is in you through the laying on of my hands, for God gave us a spirit not of fear but of power and love and self-control" (2 Timothy 1:6–7).

What does Paul mean by "fan into flame"?

We have a wood-burning fireplace, and our family loves to have a fire when we settle into the living room to watch a movie or read. Because we live in the northeast, we have ample opportunities to do so. If I can't have warmer weather, at least I can have almost year-round fires. You know how it goes when you build a fire—you place the logs in the fireplace, add newspaper, and light it on fire. But once you get the fire going, you can't walk away and assume

201

it will keep burning. You have to be intentional. Sometimes you have to fan it to keep it going or make it hotter. Neglecting the fire will cause it to flame out.

Likewise, we should be intentional in fanning into flame the Spirit inside us—"a Spirit *not* of fear but of power and love and self-control" (2 Timothy 1:7, emphasis added). Let's look at the benefits of heeding Paul's instruction.

A Spirit of Power

The "Spirit of power" Paul writes about is not our spirit. It's the all-powerful person of the Holy Spirit. The Greek word for power in this verse is *dunamis*, from which we get the words *dynamite* and *dynamic*. This is extraordinary power producing vibrant followers of Jesus.

The "Spirit of power" frees us from slavery to fear. Spirit-generated power makes us fearless in facing our battles and in sharing the hope of Jesus.

Have you witnessed the fearlessness of a Spirit-filled person? I have a friend who passed away recently from cancer, but in her battle, she was so full of the Holy Spirit and so utterly fearless of the future. The Spirit emboldened her to witness to God's goodness in her suffering, and countless hearts were opened to the Gospel through her story and the power of the Spirit. But we don't have to be battling a life-threatening disease to experience very real fear.

> The "Spirit of power" frees us from slavery to fear.

I'm actually being hit with an unusual amount of fear right now. Fear over decisions we're making, fear over things our kids are facing, fear over uncertainty of what's coming, fear of not measuring up to expectations, and fear of failure. I don't think of myself as a fearful person, so I didn't even realize how much fear is gripping me until this moment. So I write this to you humbly: When fear tries to grip us, let's call aloud on the power of the Spirit inside us! I'm pausing here to pray with you now, "Jesus, make me fearless in your faithfulness!"

I also don't mean to simplify the complexity of fear in our lives and the power it holds over us. There are very practical steps we must take and help we must get when our lives are paralyzed by fear. But I do want to encourage us not to neglect the Spirit's role in transforming us into fearless people who trust in the sovereignty and goodness of God. The more we learn to live in the assurance that "the one who is in you is greater than the one who is in the world" (1 John 4:4 NIV), the more fearless we can become.

A Spirit of Love

Now let's look at the "Spirit of love" God has given us. See, the Holy Spirit doesn't just have love; He is love and He manifests love in our lives. This is *agape* love—the highest expression of love. And as hard as we might try to define or describe this love, it remains inexpressibly greater than we can imagine.

The Spirit enables us "to know and to believe the love that God has for us,"[2] and this perfect love drives out fear in our lives, because when we know the utterly for-us nature of God's love, we are empowered to trust Him in whatever may come.

More so, Jesus said love should be the defining characteristic of His children, and He wasn't talking about self-generated love. Spirit-generated love in our lives is what makes the Gospel contagious. Think about this—of all the ways Jesus could have said the world would know we are His disciples, He chose love (John 13:35).

Spirit-generated love is pure, sacrificial, radical love that points to the sacrificial love of Jesus. When we are lacking love, we know we are lacking the fullness of the Spirit, and we need to yield to His authority. The only way to have greater love flow from our lives is to ask the Holy Spirit to become larger in our life. We need Him to flood every room in our heart.

A Spirit of Self-Control

Finally, let's look at the "Spirit of self-control" God has given us. I take great encouragement knowing that the Holy Spirit *in* me is able to produce self-control *from* me.

Where do you need more self-control? If you've read my previous books, you know that self-control, particularly in my role as a mom, is something I've needed God to supernaturally create in me. I never knew how angry I could get—or how loud I could yell—until I became a mom. This is the secret shame so many parents carry.

But knowing I have the Spirit of self-control inside me assures me I have been enabled to choose gentleness and kindness in my words and tone, which I can exercise when I am yielded to Him. This is not feel-good fluff. This is the real stuff, and it's changing me. Have I arrived? Definitely not. It's a process that the Spirit will continue and bring to completion when Jesus returns (Philippians 1:6). But the growth is real and good.

> He wants to give you self-control in every circumstance where you feel out of control.

Maybe you need the Holy Spirit's supernatural self-control to be victorious over an addiction or sin or something you run to in order to numb. Maybe it's substances, shopping, scrolling social media for affirmation, sex outside of God's best, or sugar and other food cravings. We all have something, because we're human! The question is, do we live powerless under it or victorious over it?

Our struggles are no match for the Holy Spirit's uncontainable power. He wants to help you live in the freedom for which Christ has set you free! He wants to give you self-control in every circumstance where you feel out of control. But you have to co-operate. And in doing so, His holy fire will emanate from within!

last but not least

Reflect: What role does fear play in your life? Where does your fear stem from?

Respond: Write down the fears you are facing. Be specific. Now speak the truth of 2 Timothy 1:7 over each one of those fears. For example, you might proclaim, "God has not given me a Spirit of fear, but of power and love and self-control, so I will faithfully trust God for/to _____." Fill in that blank to address each specific fear. Then, close in prayer: "God, thank you for your Spirit of fearlessness within me, enabling me to live in the victory you have secured for me."

twenty-nine

He Champions Us

I remember a season when I was so exhausted and overwhelmed that I couldn't even mutter my prayers aloud, and I fell asleep every time I attempted to pray in silence. I was nursing a newborn who didn't sleep, while also trying to parent our three older boys who were eight, ten, and twelve. But still, on Sunday mornings, we somehow wrangled our whole crew into the car and made our way to church because I desperately needed to be in an atmosphere of worship and allow hope to rise in my soul.

One Sunday after worship, when I must have been looking especially wrecked, I was on my way out the door when I ran into a friend who serves on the prayer team. She asked if she could come by the house and pray for me. Tears filled my eyes, and she knew that my tears were saying, "Yes, please, *yes*" before I even spoke a word.

The following Tuesday she stopped by the house, and when she asked me if there was anything specific she could pray for, the floodgates opened. I struggled to speak through my sobbing, "I don't even know. Anything!" "It's okay, the Holy Spirit knows what you need," she assured me, and she began to pray.

My friend welcomed the Holy Spirit's prayers on my behalf, and I settled into the hope and strength of God that filled me in that time of prayer. While I didn't turn into Superwoman, I did have a renewed sense of provision that I knew was from the Holy Spirit, and that was more than enough to carry me through those sleepless days.

What my friend demonstrated that day was the biblical truth that the Holy Spirit helps us in our weakness. Paul writes about the way the Holy Spirit does this in Romans 8:23, 26–27 (NIV):

> Not only so, but we ourselves, who have the firstfruits of the Spirit, groan inwardly as we wait eagerly for our adoption to sonship, the redemption of our bodies. . . . In the same way, the Spirit helps us in our weakness. We do not know what we ought to pray for, but the Spirit himself intercedes for us through wordless groans. And he who searches our hearts knows the mind of the Spirit, because the Spirit intercedes for God's people in accordance with the will of God.

We can take immense encouragement from the truth that the Holy Spirit is championing us in our weakness.

When I Am Weak, I Am Strong

One of the greatest things about knowing the strength of God is the freedom to admit we are weak. There is so much pressure in our culture to pretend our flesh is strong enough to face what this life throws our way. But as Paul taught in 2 Corinthians 12, when we confess we are weak in the flesh, we are made strong in the Spirit. Said differently, when we trust the sufficiency of God's strength, the pressure to pretend we are something we aren't is lifted, and the Spirit's power becomes undeniably real in our lives.

This doesn't mean God removes weakness from us. It's so much better than that. It means He gives us the help of His Spirit *in* it. We

207

get to (get to!) experience the power of God through our weakness. It is a power that far exceeds any strength we find in ourselves.

As A. W. Tozer said, "God is looking for people through whom He can do the impossible—what a pity that we plan only things we can do by ourselves."[1]

When you find yourself in situations where you're saying, "I can't do this. I don't have what it takes. I don't have the courage. I don't have the energy. I don't have the strength," take heart and hear the Holy Spirit saying, "I've got this! I've got you!"

He Groans for Me

But there's more to glean from this passage about how the Holy Spirit champions us. Paul says the Holy Spirit prays for us! This is an incredible benefit for those of us who see the many deficiencies in our prayer life. When we don't know what to say or what to ask for or we get distracted and, dare we admit it, even bored, because we forget what a privilege prayer is, we can confidently trust that the Holy Spirit has us covered. Even better, He steps in to pray for things we don't even know we need or want!

> The needs nestled in our hearts that we don't know how to articulate become the cry of the Spirit on our behalf.

Maybe you're feeling a little bit like I did on the day my friend came over to pray for me. Just empty, like there is nothing left. Maybe your heart is too torn up to tell the Lord what you need. Or maybe you have a heavy heart over decisions you have to make and you're afraid to pray for the wrong thing. Perhaps you doubt your prayers even matter or have power.

Take courage, my friend, because the Holy Spirit prays on your behalf. The needs nestled in *our* hearts that we don't know how to articulate become the cry of the Spirit on our behalf.

The Spirit "makes our groaning *His* groaning, putting His prayers to the Father inside our prayers. . . . In every specific request, then, the Father hears us praying for what is both truly best for us, and pleasing to Him, 'and the intercession of the Spirit is answered as God works all things for our good.'"[2]

What joy should fill our soul when we sit in the assurance that the Holy Spirit's appeal on our behalf is very personal! He knows our frustrations and He knows our longings, and He knows we need help praying in accordance with God's will and discerning God's ways. So He takes the cries of our hearts—our groans—and goes to God on our behalf. As the Holy Spirit groans for you in perfect accordance with God's will, God discerns His wordless prayers perfectly.

> The way God works all things for our good is by conforming us "to the image of his Son."

So Jesus—who sits at the right hand of God Almighty—is interceding for you, and the Holy Spirit who dwells within you is also interceding for you. Look what we've been given. Look who we have in our corner!

Paul concludes with confidence, "And we know that in all things God works for the good of those who love him, who have been called according to his purpose" (Romans 8:28 NIV). Even through the Spirit's prayers for us, His sanctifying power is at work, because the way God works all things for our good is by conforming us "to the image of his Son" (v. 29). The Spirit's prayer is that whatever we endure would draw us closer to Jesus and make us more like Him.

Of course, knowing this benefit of having the Holy Spirit isn't an excuse to be lazy in our prayer life. Learning how to pray the Scriptures is an essential and enjoyable part of our walk with Christ, but let us remember with confidence that the Holy Spirit is always helping us along.

To Whom Do I Pray?

The beautiful trinitarian nature of prayer is that we pray to the Father, through His Son, in the Spirit's power.

Jesus taught us how to pray in Matthew 6:9 when He told His disciples, "Pray then like this: Our Father in heaven."

Because of Jesus, we have the miraculous privilege of praying to the Father. And we pray in Jesus' name because He is our High Priest whose sacrifice gives us unlimited and unrestricted access (see Hebrews 4:14–16). Jesus, who is able to sympathize with our weakness and suffering, yet is without sin, makes it possible for us to draw near to the throne of God, the throne of grace.

And while we won't find any prayers addressed to the Holy Spirit in Scripture, Paul teaches us to pray "at all times in the Spirit" (Ephesians 6:18). The Spirit is the One who inclines us to pray and also prays on our behalf. We need His guidance in our prayer life and His groaning on our behalf, all for God's glory.

With that structure in mind, one could easily wonder if that means we should address our prayers only to the Father. That would be a firm no. We can talk directly to Jesus and the Holy Spirit in prayer. In fact, it should be our aim to be in continual communication and communion with the Three-In-One.

"Holy Spirit, help!" is a powerful and poignant prayer. "Thank you, Jesus" is one I whisper often. And that is just the beginning of the conversation. While keeping in mind the pattern of prayer in the New Testament, we can commune with the Father, the Son, and the Holy Spirit. There is no competition for our attention among them.

So friend, I might not know what burdens you carry today, or what worries wake you up at night, but I do know that the Holy Spirit is at work on your behalf, strengthening you and praying—even pleading—for the Father's will to be done in you. He takes your midnight worries before the throne of God and champions you to the Father. Let your soul settle into this matchless work of the Spirit!

last but not least

Reflect: What, if anything, makes you uncomfortable with the idea of confessing you are weak in the flesh and in need of supernatural strength? When have you experienced the championing of the Holy Spirit in your weakness, perhaps through the manifestation of His power or through the assurance of His petitions?

Respond: Thank the Holy Spirit for tucking His prayers into yours, in accordance with God's will. If you don't keep a prayer journal, consider starting one today. As you do this, remember that when you don't know what to say or how to pray, the Spirit has your back. And as you record your prayers in the days and weeks ahead, don't forget to look back over previous entries to notice how God has been faithful to answer those prayers!

thirty

He's the Friend We All Need

As I've mentioned before, I am writing this book in the peak of the global pandemic, an apex where fear and anxiety and loss have consumed the conversation. We have been forced to face the frailty and uncertainty of this life. But the perfection and certainty of the glory that awaits us beyond this earthly groaning has also been highlighted because people are searching for a hope and security that can't be found outside of Jesus.

What we're experiencing globally makes me think about other periods of great suffering, and I'm reminded of a story told by Corrie ten Boom—a woman who has certainly endured the depths of suffering.

Corrie ten Boom was a Dutch Christian woman who was sent to a Nazi concentration camp at the age of fifty-two alongside her sister and her father. Their "crime" was hiding Jewish people in their home to help them escape Nazi Germany.

But long before her days in the concentration camp, as just a little girl, Corrie read about martyrs for the Christian faith, and wondered if she'd have the courage to suffer for Jesus like they did, as she shared in a letter decades later:

"Daddy, I am afraid that I will never be strong enough to be a martyr for Jesus Christ."

"Tell me," said Father, "when you take a train trip to Amsterdam, when do I give you the money for the ticket? Three weeks before?"

"No, Daddy, you give me the money for the ticket just before we get on the train."

"That's right," my father said, "and so it is with God's strength. Our Father in Heaven knows when you will need the strength to be a martyr for Jesus Christ. He will supply all you need—just in time."[1]

Corrie concluded in that same letter, "Betsy and I were prisoners for the Lord, we were so weak, but we got power because the Holy Spirit was on us. That mighty inner strengthening of the Holy Spirit helped us through. No, you will not be strong in yourself when the tribulation comes. Rather, you will be strong in the power of Him who will not forsake you. For seventy-six years I have known the Lord Jesus and not once has He ever left me or let me down."[2]

The suffering—and strengthening—Corrie ten Boom speaks of is what the apostle Peter wrote about: "Beloved, do not be surprised at the fiery trial when it comes upon you to test you, as though something strange were happening to you. But rejoice insofar as you share Christ's sufferings, that you may also rejoice and be glad when his glory is revealed. If you are insulted for the name of Christ, you are blessed, because the Spirit of glory and of God rests upon you" (1 Peter 4:12–14).

The Spirit of Glory

If you suffer, "you are blessed," Peter writes. Let's be honest. We don't tend to equate our suffering with blessing. If anything, suffering feels like we've been forsaken. So why would Paul be so bold as to suggest that we are blessed when we walk through fiery trials? Because even as you endure hardship and suffering, the Holy Spirit, the "Spirit of glory," is upon your life and will call you into eternal glory in Christ (1 Peter 5:10–11).

We may not be prisoners for the Lord, as Corrie ten Boom was, but we will certainly know suffering in its various forms in this life. We cannot avoid it, and Jesus warned us of it, but this is certain: We never walk alone through it and we are never without hope as we endure it. The Spirit of glory applies the hope of glory in our suffering.

> The Spirit of glory applies the hope of glory in our suffering.

The breathtaking promise is that the Holy Spirit will carry us through every valley, every trial, and every ounce of suffering, right into the arms of God. He does this through His intercession *for* us, through the comfort of His presence *in* us, and through the hope that He makes abound in us.

I would echo the words of ten Boom, that God the Father, God the Son, and God the Holy Spirit have never left me or let me down. They are altogether trustworthy and better than we could ever imagine.

Faithful from before time began, they love us and lead us in perfect unity. And nothing *has* ever, or *will* ever, be able to separate us from their perfect love (Romans 8:38–39).

He Is *for* You

Do you have a friend you can count on to champion you all the way to the finish line? A friend who is just so *for* you? A friend who is eager for you to know your potential and use your gifts? A friend who fights for your mind to know the truth of who you are in Jesus and how loved you are by Him when doubts creep in and feelings of unworthiness try to settle in your heart? A friend who knows your weaknesses and comes alongside you to help carry your burdens when life feels too heavy? A friend you know will never forsake you?

Several names quickly come to my mind—and for that I am so very grateful! But the friend who has known me longer than any other is Morella, whom I fondly call Moe. We met in Sunday school when I was eight years old, and she has always been the friend I am most myself with. I am completely me with Moe. I could go on and on about what I love about Moe (like the fact that she introduced me to the love of my life!), but this I will tell you: She is so incredibly loyal. I am never afraid of losing her companionship and I know she is always cheering me on. I know that nothing will make Moe give up on me.

I pray that you have a friend like Moe, but no matter where you find yourself in earthly friendships, I want you to know you have that kind of friend—and so much more—in the person of the Holy Spirit. The benefits of His friendship are beyond comprehension.

He knows you better than you know yourself, and He is *for* you. He wants to help you enjoy all of your spiritual blessings in Christ. He wants to develop the gifts God has stored in you. He wants to fill your mind with life-giving truth and guide you according to God's will for your life. He wants to speak *to* you and *through* you. He wants to empower you to live right and bear fruit. He wants to infuse intimacy into your relationship with Jesus.

> The benefits of His friendship are beyond comprehension.

The Holy Spirit wants you to know the welling-up of joy that overflows from being filled with Him. He wants you to lean on His loyal companionship, to experience His tender comfort in suffering and His unshakeable hope in hardship. He wants you to know the love that can only be found in Jesus. He wants you to know He is in your corner and can be counted on! He wants you to have victory over sin and freedom from the sting of shame. He wants you to fulfill the purpose for which you were created, for the glory of God!

Let these truths settle on you and ignite a fire in your soul!

Oh, sister, I am so glad we didn't miss out on discovering how life is so much better with the Holy Spirit. We weren't made to do this life on our own. We were created to live INpowered by the Holy Spirit.

last but not least

Reflect: I can't help but wonder, after everything we've discovered together, if there are specific attributes of the Holy Spirit, or particular benefits of His presence, that stand out to you? For instance, if you were to fill in the blank below, what would you write?

Respond: My favorite thing(s) about the Holy Spirit is/are _____ _____. Don't hold back!

Personal Closing Note

For my husband's birthday, I may not have been able to surprise him with a trip to Israel, as I mentioned earlier, but I was able to throw a small surprise party for him during a time when COVID prevented large gatherings. I had a few of his local friends surprise him for a round of golf, which was followed by dinner with the wives on the restaurant patio at the course.

During the dinner, Mike's friends took turns at the mic, telling moving stories of how he has profoundly impacted their lives. I have to tell you, I'm always proud to be his wife, but it was especially true on this night.

The last one to speak was Andre, our son from Haiti. He shared about how he grew up in an orphanage where he had the love of several women, all of whom he proudly calls Mom. But then he explained this: Oftentimes in life we don't know how much we have missed out on something until we actually have it. We can assume something might be really good, like the way a certain food might taste or the way a certain vacation might feel, but until we actually experience it, we don't really know. Then he said, "I didn't know how much I missed out on having a father's love until Mike called me his son. I had assumptions about how it would feel to have the love of a father, but I didn't really know. But now I know, and it's even better than I thought it would be." As you can imagine, there wasn't a dry eye on that outdoor patio.

I resonated with what Andre said because it was similar to how I have felt about my new enjoyment of the Holy Spirit's presence in my life. I didn't know how much I was missing out on until I began to really experience it. And it's more than I imagined.

So this is my wholehearted prayer for us: that we would unabashedly welcome the activity of God the Father, God the Son, and God the Holy Spirit in our lives. May the Spirit bubble up a joy so uncontainable and light a fire so fierce inside us that everyone we encounter would say to us what they said to the disciples after Pentecost—"I want what you have!" And may our aim be the same as theirs—"By the power of the Spirit inside me, let me tell you about my Jesus!"

Thank you for joining me on this remarkable journey!

Now to him who is able to do far more abundantly than all that we ask or think, according to the power at work within us.

Ephesians 3:20

Your friend,

Jeannie

Acknowledgments

I remember exactly where I was sitting when I found the courage to call my agent, Andrew Wolgemuth, to say, "I need to tell you what is stirring in my spirit for my next book, and I need you to tell me it's a very bad idea. I need you to tell me nobody will want to read this book and I should keep it to myself." But instead, he responded enthusiastically. A few days later he got back to me, after sharing the idea with the Wolgemuth team, and he replied along the lines of, "We believe women don't only *need* this book. We believe they will *want* this book! And you are the right person to write it. I am behind you all the way." Andrew, your partnership has been a priceless gift, and I'm immensely grateful for the way you champion my work in the most Christlike way. It's a privilege to be represented by you.

Jennifer Dukes Lee, where do I begin? How kind of the Holy Spirit to make it undeniably clear to me that you were the perfect editor for this project. Thank you for believing in this book so wholeheartedly and for helping me believe this is a book that will deeply resonate with women today. Your wisdom, wonderful gift of storytelling, wild love for Jesus, and brilliant editorial skills made this book far more than I ever dreamed it would be. Your thoughtful care on this project, both as an editor and a friend, made the whole process so enjoyable.

Thank you to the entire Bethany House team. You have been wonderful to work with. I am thankful for the integrity and intentionality of the team. Sharon Hodge, thank you for your keen editorial work on this book. You were so thoughtful and thorough, and I'm so grateful. Deirdre and the marketing team, thank you for being so committed to ensuring the marketing reflects the heartbeat of this book.

To Joel Muddamalle, director of theology at Proverbs 31 Ministries and now my dear friend, thank you for partnering with me and providing such a helpful theological review of the book. As you know, my greatest desire and utmost priority was to, as accurately as any human being can, write a solid biblical book about the Holy Spirit. Thank you for the lively conversations and the thorough review to ensure we are offering a book that is deeply grounded in God's Word. That's amazing!

To Ben Valentine and Blaze Robertson, both pastors and dear friends, thank you for your willingness to read the manuscript in its final stages and offer such helpful and encouraging feedback. I'm so grateful!

Jodie Berndt, the four days we spent on our writer's retreat at your home was the catalyst I needed to believe God would give me the wisdom and words to write this book. Those Spirit-filled hours of prayer and writing and conversation and laughter and chocolate-eating were such a gift to me. Your friendship is pure grace. Thank you for being both a mentor and cherished friend.

Courtney DeFeo and Paula Faris, can we talk about how endlessly patient and outrageously loving you both were as we spent hours (and days and weeks) on the lake brainstorming about this book? Court, the way you champion people inspires me. Being generous, hilarious, wildly encouraging, and unbelievably creative are just a few of the things that make you so darn amazing. Thank you for being TIRELESS in helping me believe I was made to write this book. I love you so! And Paula Faris, how fast can a friendship grow? Oh, we know. Sister, you make my heart so happy. You're the friend who faithfully shows up—oftentimes with a fountain Coke—even if it's on FaceTime. You spurred me on in the writing of this book in ways I will never be able to adequately explain. I can't wait to see what God has planned next for #WUHQ. Love you, girl!

To my wonderfully supportive in-laws, Gail and Tony Cunnion. Thank you for your support and encouragement and affirmation as I've written this book. Knowing you are cheering for me means the world, and I'm so grateful! I love you both.

Deep gratitude and so much love to the friends who gather around the kitchen island, travel to Haiti, or just love one another hard on the daily: Julia Eberwein, Desi Robertson, Lindsay Snedeker, Nicole Zasowski, Laura Boone, and Angela Kilcullen. Nobody better to do life with than you!

Ami McConnell, thank you for being excited about this book from the moment I shared it with you. I lean on your confidence in me, or better said, your confidence in the Jesus in me. I adore you!

To the soul sister who I know always has my back and will always point me to Jesus, Elisabeth Hasselbeck. Fiercely loyal and loving, and the loudest cheerleader of others, you inspire me in innumerable ways. I love you, E. #Godjustknew

And to Morella Atkinson, you only need to turn to chapter 30 to read all the things. Thank you for loving me the longest and for your unfailing friendship. We really are "stuck together with God's glue." I love you, Moe.

To my sisters, Patti Callahan Henry and Barbi Burris—you make me believe I can do anything. Is that a sister superpower? It must be. What would I do without you? I don't want to know. I love you beyond.

Mom and Dad, this book is, in many ways, your fault ☺. You faithfully led a church that didn't shy away from teaching about and welcoming the Holy Spirit's power and presence in our lives today. Your vibrant and authentic relationship with Jesus made me want to know Him and love Him all the more. And when I stumbled, you never shamed or abandoned. Yeah, you reflected the Father's heart over and over again. And when I felt God nudging me to write this book, you were the first ones I called to ask, "Where should I begin if I want to dive deep into studying the Holy Spirit?" You cheered me on and prayed for me as I wrote, and you joyfully read every word so we could wrestle with the harder things. Thank you for all the ways you love and support me, but more than anything, thank you for giving me Jesus.

To Hubby—my best friend and the best thing that ever happened to me. I saw Jesus in you the moment I laid eyes on you, but for the last seventeen years I have watched you fall deeper and deeper in love with Him, I have watched you grow more and more dependent on His faithfulness, and I have watched you become more and more amazed by His goodness. And all of this has been profoundly impactful in my own walk with God. You lean on the Holy Spirit to lead you, and this gives me such confidence in how you lead our family. You take such good care of us. You have this beautiful tenderness to the Spirit of God, and it inspires me to live more in step with Him. You model for our boys a genuine love for Jesus in how you pursue Him daily, and you intentionally instruct them in a grace-filled way of life. You are humble and kind, and strong and courageous, and I'm so blessed to be called "mine" by you. I love you, Mike Cunnion, and I have no doubt that I absolutely take for granted all the ways you support me and affirm God's calling on my life. I would never have the courage to keep writing without you continually reminding me that God will always give me what I need to do what He's called me to do.

Boys, good grief, I love being your mom. Cal, Brennan, Owen, Finn, and Andre—I'll never get over how generous it was of God to entrust the five of you to your dad and me. Of all the things God welcomes me to do, being your mama is my highest privilege and my greatest joy. You fill our home with so much love and laughter, and with you is my favorite place to be. As the sign in our kitchen reads, and as I pray over you each day, "'I pray that Christ may live in your hearts by faith. I pray that you will be filled with love. I pray that you will be able to understand how wide and how long and how high and how deep His love is. I pray that you will know the love of Christ. His love goes beyond anything we can understand. I pray that you will be filled with God Himself' (Ephesians 3:17–19)." May you be ever aware of the constant companionship and unlimited power of the Holy Spirit inside you to help you continue to grow into the extraordinary men God made you to be! I love you with my whole heart.

Lord, I am in awe of you. Your love undoes me. It overwhelms me. How is it that you don't give up on me? A grace so great I can't comprehend it, but I will use every last breath you grant me to tell the world about the hope we have in Jesus. Lord, I just thank you for welcoming us into deeper intimacy with you through your Spirit and for inviting me to write a book to tell of it. How is it that you would choose to take up residence in us so that we would never be alone or without everything we need to live the free and full life Jesus purchased for us on the cross? This book is a love offering to you, Father. Let it bring you all the praise and let it draw your daughters into deeper love with Jesus and greater dependence on your Spirit. I love you, Lord.

Appendix

Spiritual Gifts Survey
LifeWay Christian Resources

Directions

This is not a test, so there are no wrong answers. The Spiritual Gifts Survey consists of eighty statements. Some items reflect concrete actions, other items are descriptive traits, and still others are statements of belief.

- Select the one response you feel best characterizes yourself, and place that number in the blank provided. Record your answer in the blank beside each item.

- Do not spend too much time on any one item. Remember, it is not a test. Usually your immediate response is best.

- Please give an answer for each item. Do not skip any items.

- Do not ask others how they are answering or how they think you should answer.

- Work at your own pace.

Your response choices are:

5—Highly characteristic of me/definitely true for me
4—Most of the time this would describe me/be true for me
3—Frequently characteristic of me/true for me—about 50 percent of the time
2—Occasionally characteristic of me/true for me—about 25 percent of the time
1—Not at all characteristic of me/definitely untrue for me

_____ 1. I have the ability to organize ideas, resources, time, and people effectively.

_____ 2. I am willing to study and prepare for the task of teaching.

_____ 3. I am able to relate the truths of God to specific situations.

_____ 4. I have a God-given ability to help others grow in their faith.

_____ 5. I possess a special ability to communicate the truth of salvation.

_____ 6. I have the ability to make critical decisions when necessary.

_____ 7. I am sensitive to the hurts of people.

_____ 8. I experience joy in meeting needs through sharing possessions.

_____ 9. I enjoy studying.

_____ 10. I have delivered God's message of warning and judgment.

_____ 11. I am able to sense the true motivation of persons and movements.

_____ 12. I have a special ability to trust God in difficult situations.

_____ 13. I have a strong desire to contribute to the establishment of new churches.

_____ 14. I take action to meet physical and practical needs rather than merely talking about or planning to help.

_____ 15. I enjoy entertaining guests in my home.

_____ 16. I can adapt my guidance to fit the maturity of those working with me.

_____ 17. I can delegate and assign meaningful work.

_____ 18. I have an ability and desire to teach.

_____ 19. I am usually able to analyze a situation correctly.

_____ 20. I have a natural tendency to encourage others.

_____ 21. I am willing to take the initiative in helping other Christians grow in their faith.

_____ 22. I have an acute awareness of the emotions of other people, such as loneliness, pain, fear, and anger.

_____ 23. I am a cheerful giver.

_____ 24. I spend time digging into facts.

_____ 25. I feel that I have a message from God to deliver to others.

_____ 26. I can recognize when a person is genuine/honest.

_____ 27. I am a person of vision (a clear mental portrait of a preferable future given by God). I am able to communicate vision in such a way that others commit to making the vision a reality.

_____ 28. I am willing to yield to God's will rather than question and waver.

_____ 29. I would like to be more active in getting the gospel to people in other lands.

_____ 30. It makes me happy to do things for people in need.

_____ 31. I am successful in getting a group to do its work joyfully.

_____ 32. I am able to make strangers feel at ease.

_____ 33. I have the ability to plan learning approaches.

_____ 34. I can identify those who need encouragement.

_____ 35. I have trained Christians to be more obedient disciples of Christ.

_____ 36. I am willing to do whatever it takes to see others come to Christ.

_____ 37. I am attracted to people who are hurting.

_____ 38. I am a generous giver.

_____ 39. I am able to discover new truths.

_____ 40. I have spiritual insights from Scripture concerning issues and people that compel me to speak out.

_____ 41. I can sense when a person is acting in accord with God's will.

_____ 42. I can trust in God even when things look dark.

_____ 43. I can determine where God wants a group to go and help it get there.

_____ 44. I have a strong desire to take the gospel to places where it has never been heard.

_____ 45. I enjoy reaching out to new people in my church and community.

_____ 46. I am sensitive to the needs of people.

_____ 47. I have been able to make effective and efficient plans for accomplishing the goals of a group.

_____ 48. I often am consulted when fellow Christians are struggling to make difficult decisions.

_____ 49. I think about how I can comfort and encourage others in my congregation.

_____ 50. I am able to give spiritual direction to others.

_____ 51. I am able to present the gospel to lost persons in such a way that they accept the Lord and His salvation.

_____ 52. I possess an unusual capacity to understand the feelings of those in distress.

_____ 53. I have a strong sense of stewardship based on the recognition that God owns all things.

_____ 54. I have delivered to other persons messages that have come directly from God.

_____ 55. I can sense when a person is acting under God's leadership.

_____ 56. I try to be in God's will continually and be available for His use.

_____ 57. I feel that I should take the gospel to people who have different beliefs from me.

_____ 58. I have an acute awareness of the physical needs of others.

_____ 59. I am skilled in setting forth positive and precise steps of action.

_____ 60. I like to meet visitors at church and make them feel welcome.

_____ 61. I explain Scripture in such a way that others understand it.

_____ 62. I can usually see spiritual solutions to problems.

_____ 63. I welcome opportunities to help people who need comfort, consolation, encouragement, and counseling.

_____ 64. I feel at ease in sharing Christ with nonbelievers.

_____ 65. I can influence others to perform to their highest God-given potential.

_____ 66. I recognize the signs of stress and distress in others.

_____ 67. I desire to give generously and unpretentiously to worthwhile projects and ministries.

_____ 68. I can organize facts into meaningful relationships.

_____ 69. God gives me messages to deliver to His people.

_____ 70. I am able to sense whether people are being honest when they tell of their religious experiences.

_____ 71. I enjoy presenting the gospel to persons of other cultures and backgrounds.

_____ 72. I enjoy doing little things that help people.

_____ 73. I can give a clear, uncomplicated presentation.

_____ 74. I have been able to apply biblical truth to the specific needs of my church.

_____ 75. God has used me to encourage others to live Christlike lives.

_____ 76. I have sensed the need to help other people become more effective in their ministries.

_____ 77. I like to talk about Jesus to those who do not know Him.

_____ 78. I have the ability to make strangers feel comfortable in my home.

_____ 79. I have a wide range of study resources and know how to secure information.

_____ 80. I feel assured that a situation will change for the glory of God even when the situation seems impossible.

Scoring Your Survey

Follow these directions to figure your score for each spiritual gift.

1. Place in each box your numerical response (1–5) to the item number that is indicated below the box.

2. For each gift, add the numbers in the boxes and put the total in the TOTAL box.

LEADERSHIP	+	+	+	+	=
Item 6	Item 16	Item 27	Item 43	Item 65	TOTAL
ADMINISTRATION					
Item 1	Item 17	Item 31	Item 47	Item 59	TOTAL
TEACHING					
Item 2	Item 18	Item 33	Item 61	Item 73	TOTAL
KNOWLEDGE					
Item 9	Item 24	Item 39	Item 68	Item 79	TOTAL
WISDOM					
Item 3	Item 19	Item 48	Item 62	Item 72	TOTAL
PROPHECY					
Item 10	Item 25	Item 40	Item 54	Item 69	TOTAL
DISCERNMENT					
Item 11	Item 26	Item 41	Item 55	Item 70	TOTAL
EXHORTATION					
Item 20	Item 34	Item 49	Item 63	Item 75	TOTAL
SHEPHERDING					
Item 4	Item 21	Item 35	Item 50	Item 76	TOTAL
FAITH					
Item 12	Item 28	Item 42	Item 56	Item 80	TOTAL
EVANGELISM					
Item 5	Item 36	Item 51	Item 64	Item 77	TOTAL
APOSTLESHIP					
Item 13	Item 29	Item 44	Item 57	Item 71	TOTAL
SERVICE/HELPS					
Item 14	Item 30	Item 46	Item 58	Item 72	TOTAL
MERCY					
Item 7	Item 22	Item 37	Item 51	Item 66	TOTAL
GIVING					
Item 8	Item 23	Item 38	Item 53	Item 67	TOTAL
HOSPITALITY					
Item 15	Item 32	Item 45	Item 60	Item 78	TOTAL

Graphing Your Profile

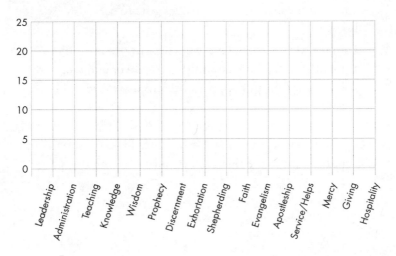

1. For each gift, place a mark across the bar at the point that corresponds to your TOTAL for that gift.
2. For each gift, shade the bar below the mark that you have drawn.
3. The resultant graph gives a picture of your gifts. Gifts for which the bars are tall are the ones in which you appear to be strongest. Gifts for which the bars are shorter are the ones in which you appear to be less strong.

Now that you have completed the survey, thoughtfully answer the following questions.

The gifts I have begun to discover in my life are:

1. _____

2. _____

3. _____

- After prayer and worship, I am beginning to sense that God wants me to use my spiritual gifts to serve Christ's body by _____.

- I am not sure yet how God wants me to use my gifts to serve others. But I am committed to prayer and worship, seeking wisdom and opportunities to use the gifts I have received from God.

Ask God to help you know how He has gifted you for service and how you can begin to use this gift in ministry to others.

Notes

Chapter 2: He Makes His Home in Us

1. Acts 2:38.
2. 1 Corinthians 12:31. More about this in chapter 27, "He Gives Us Spiritual Gifts."
3. Billy Graham, *The Holy Spirit: Activating God's Power in Your Life* (Nashville, TN: Thomas Nelson, 1978), 32.
4. "Lexicon :: Strong's G3875—parakletos," *Blue Letter Bible*, https://www .blueletterbible.org/lang/lexicon/lexicon.cfm?t=kjv&strongs=g3875.
5. "Allon," R. Kent Hughes, *John: That You May Believe, Preaching the Word* (Wheaton, IL: Crossway Books, 1999), 342–344.
6. Timothy Keller, *Encounters with Jesus: Unexpected Answers to Life's Biggest Questions* (New York: Penguin Books, 2015), 141.
7. D. Martyn Lloyd-Jones, *Life in Christ: Studies in 1 John* (Wheaton, IL: Crossway, 2002), 386.

Chapter 3: He Never Leaves Us

1. Dr. Seuss, *Oh, the Places You'll Go!* (New York, NY: Random House, 1990), n.p.
2. See 1 Samuel 15.
3. Dr. Frank John Ninivaggi, "Loneliness: A New Epidemic in the USA," *Psychology Today*, February 12, 2019, https://www.psychologytoday.com/us/blog /envy/201902/loneliness-new-epidemic-in-the-usa.
4. Neil Howe, "Millennials and the Loneliness Epidemic," *Forbes*, May 3, 2019, https://www.forbes.com/sites/neilhowe/2019/05/03/millennials-and-the-loneliness -epidemic/#7dcecfa87676.

Chapter 4: He Is God

1. Billy Graham, *The Holy Spirit: Activating God's Power in Your Life* (Nashville, TN: Thomas Nelson, 1978), 10.
2. Tony Evans, *Time to Get Serious* (Wheaton, IL: Crossway, 1995), 22.
3. R. T. Kendall, *Holy Fire: A Balanced, Biblical Look at the Holy Spirit's Work in Our Lives* (Lake Mary, FL: Charisma House, 2014), 13.
4. J. I. Packer, *Keep in Step with the Spirit: Finding Fullness in Our Walk with God* (Grand Rapids, MI: Baker Books, 2005), 15.

Chapter 5: He Is a Person

1. R. T. Kendall, *Holy Fire: A Balanced Biblical Look at the Holy Spirit's Work in Our Lives* (Lake Mary, FL: Charisma House, 2014), 84.
2. Kendall, *Holy Fire*, 19.

Chapter 6: He Is Equal

1. Augustine of Hippo, *The Trinity*, ed. Hermigild Dressler, trans. Stephen McKenna, vol. 45, The Fathers of the Church (Washington, DC: The Catholic University of America Press, 1963), 11.
2. Francis Chan, *Forgotten God: Reversing Our Tragic Neglect of the Holy Spirit* (Colorado Springs, CO: David C. Cook, 2009), 27.
3. Billy Graham, *The Holy Spirit: Activating God's Power in Your Life* (Nashville, TN: Thomas Nelson, 1978), xii.
4. Robert Morris, *The God I Never Knew: How Real Friendship with the Holy Spirit Can Change Your Life* (Colorado Springs, CO: Waterbrook, 2011), 116.

Chapter 7: He Is Better Than Self-Help

1. Jennie Allen, *Get Out of Your Head: Stopping the Spiral of Toxic Thoughts* (Colorado Springs, CO: Waterbrook, 2020), 57.

Chapter 8: He Is Our Guarantee

1. ESV Gospel Transformation Bible, Commentary on Matthew 12:31–32 (Wheaton, IL: Crossway, 2011), 1287.
2. R. T. Kendall, *Holy Fire: A Balanced Biblical Look at the Holy Spirit's Work in Our Lives* (Lake Mary, FL: Charisma House, 2014), 26.

Chapter 9: He Makes Much of Jesus

1. Tim Keller, *The Meaning of Marriage: Facing the Complexities of Commitment with the Wisdom of God* (New York: Penguin Books, 2013), 51.
2. R. T. Kendall, *Holy Fire: A Balanced Biblical Look at the Holy Spirit's Work in Our Lives* (Lake Mary, FL: Charisma House, 2014), 26.

Chapter 10: He Authored the Bible

1. 2 Peter 1:20–21.

2. No author is noted for this prayer found at various websites. This version was found at "Morning Prayer," *Beliefnet*, Beliefnet.com, https://www.beliefnet.com/prayers/protestant/morning/morning-prayer.aspx.

3. Tim Keller, "Son Bought and Spirit Brought," *Daily Keller: Wisdom from Keller 365 Days a Year*, October 8, 2017, http://dailykeller.com/son-bought-and-spirit-brought/.

Chapter 13: He Gave Power to Peter

1. *Baptism* here means "baptized into the family of Christ through salvation." Peter is not suggesting that water baptism is necessary for salvation. More on that later.

2. Ann Graham Lotz, *Jesus in Me: Experiencing the Holy Spirit as a Constant Companion* (Colorado Springs, CO: Multnomah, 2019), 91.

Chapter 17: He Communicates Through Us

1. John Piper, "God Will Give You Something to Say," *Desiring God*, December 27, 2016, https://www.desiringgod.org/articles/god-will-give-you-something-to-say.

2. Galatians 5:1 NIV.

Chapter 20: He Helps Us Live in Freedom

1. Jennie Allen, *Get Out of Your Head: Stopping the Spiral of Toxic Thoughts* (Colorado Springs, CO: Waterbrook, 2020), 10–11.

2. Allen, *Get Out of Your Head*, 40.

Chapter 21: He Empowers Us to Obey

1. Joel Muddamalle is the director of theology at Proverbs 31 Ministries, and this was an idea he shared with me in conversation about this passage.

2. Francis Chan, *Forgotten God: Reversing Our Tragic Neglect of the Holy Spirit* (Colorado Springs, CO: David C. Cook, 2009), 129.

Chapter 22: He Makes Us More Like Jesus

1. Meshali Mitchell, "A House God Is Building," *Meshali*, https://meshali.co/ahgib.

2. "37. hagiazó," Strong's Concordance, *Bible Hub*, Biblehub.com, https://biblehub.com/greek/37.htm.

Chapter 23: He Produces Fruit in Our Lives

1. Jodie Berndt, text message to Jeannie Cunnion, May 2020. Used by permission.

2. ESV Gospel Transformation Bible, Commentary on John 15 (Wheaton, IL: Crossway, 2011), 1436.

Chapter 24: He Fills Us

1. Chris Tomlin, "We Fall Down," © Copyright 1998, worshiptogether.com Songs (ASCAP) (admin. by EMI CMG Publishing).
2. Tim Keller, "Spirit-Filled," *Daily Keller: Wisdom from Keller 365 Days a Year*, http://dailykeller.com/spirit-filled/, January 2015.
3. Catherine Marshall, *The Helper* (Grand Rapids, MI: Chosen Books, 1978), 127.
4. John Bloom, "Lord, Fill Me with Your Spirit," *Desiring God*, January 31, 2017, https://www.desiringgod.org/articles/lord-fill-me-with-your-spirit.

Chapter 25: He Keeps Filling Us

1. J. Goetzmann, "Μετάνοια," eds. Lothar Coenen, Erich Beyreuther, and Hans Bietenhard, *New International Dictionary of New Testament Theology* (Grand Rapids, MI: Zondervan, 1986), 357.
2. John Piper, "How to Seek the Holy Spirit," *Desiring God*, January 15, 2018, https://www.desiringgod.org/messages/how-to-seek-the-holy-spirit.

Chapter 26: He Baptizes Us

1. The four references for the Gospels are Matthew 3:11; Mark 1:8; Luke 3:16; and John 1:33.
2. R. T. Kendall, *Holy Fire: A Balanced Biblical Look at the Holy Spirit's Work in Our Lives* (Lake Mary, FL: Charisma House, 2014), 133.
3. John Piper, "What Is the Baptism of the Holy Spirit?" YouTube Video, 14:06, June 2019, https://www.youtube.com/watch?v=fafWocaLTr0&list=PLFF7F6AE 365DA3564&index=31&app=desktop.
4. Piper, "What Is the Baptism of the Holy Spirit?"

Chapter 27: He Gives Us Spiritual Gifts

1. "5486. Charisma," Strong's Concordance, *Bible Hub*, Biblehub.com, https://biblehub.com/str/greek/5486.htm.

Chapter 28: He Can Be Quenched

1. Priscilla Shirer, "Fire Fall Down," *Jewelry Box*, GoingBeyond.com, March 1, 2020, https://www.goingbeyond.com/jewelry-box/fire-fall-down/.
2. 1 John 4:16.

Chapter 29: He Champions Us

1. As quoted in John C. Maxwell, *The 21 Most Powerful Minutes in a Leader's Day* (Nashville, TN: Thomas Nelson, 2007), 27.
2. Tim Keller, *Prayer: Experiencing Awe and Intimacy with God* (New York: Penguin, 2016), 72–73.

Chapter 30: He's the Friend We All Need

1. Corrie ten Boom, letter of 1974, as quoted in "Corrie ten Boom and the Rapture," *Showing Ourselves Approved*, February 19, 2019, https://soappsite .wordpress.com/2019/02/19/corrie-ten-boom-and-the-rapture-this-is-from-a-let-ter-corrie-wrote-in-1974/.

2. Ten Boom in "Corrie ten Boom and the Rapture."

Jeannie Cunnion is an author who is well-known for writing stories that make much of the wild love of Jesus because of how her life has been rescued by it. She is also a beloved Bible teacher and sought-after speaker who has been featured on outlets such as the *TODAY* show, *Fox News*, *The 700 Club*, and *Focus on the Family*. Jeannie, who holds a master's degree in social work, worked as a counselor and trainer in the adoption field before writing. She is a wife to Mike and a mama to five boys she is crazy about. Her hobbies include grocery shopping—because, five boys—and praying—because again, five boys. When not cheering for her boys on the sidelines, you'll most likely find her singing worship music off-key in her kitchen while trying not to burn dinner again. To know Jeannie is to know her deep love for Danita's Children's Home in Haiti. Jeannie would love to connect with you at www.JeannieCunnion.com.

To download discussion questions for your group
or book club, visit JeannieCunnion.com.

 Instagram @JeannieCunnion

 Facebook @JeannieCunnion

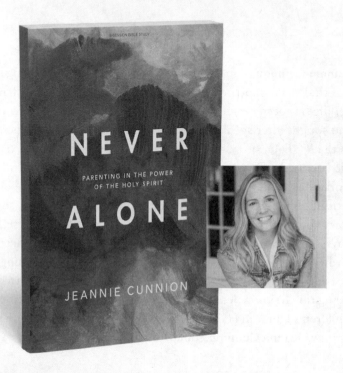